TRUE CRIME
GANGSTERS

D0177264

ASPEN BOOKS

© Aspen Books, 2018

All rights reserved. No part of this publication may be reproduced, stored in a retrieval system or transmitted, in any form or by any means, electronic, mechanical, photocopying, recording or otherwise, without prior permission in writing from the publisher.

First published in 2018.

A catalogue record for this book is available from the British Library.

ISBN: 978-1-912456-14-7

Published by Aspen Books, an imprint of Pillar Box Red Publishing Ltd.

Printed in India.

TRUE CRIME

GANGSTERS

From The Case Files of the

Claire Welch

Contents

Incidents

Introduction

When Sicily, the largest island in the Mediterranean Sea, was colonized by the Greeks in around 750 BC many important settlements were formed. Its politics became intertwined with that of Greece and the island became a "power base" on a number of occasions. When the Greeks looked for peace with the Roman Republic in 262 BC, the island eventually became the first Roman province outside of Italy. Sicily remained largely Greek but held great importance for the Romans, who used the island as the empire's granary. For 700 years, the island was a solid part of the Roman Empire, but other cultures, including the Byzantines, tried to conquer Sicily as the empire began to slowly crumble. By 965, the Arabs had taken Sicily and a reign of persecution and terror saw Sicilians fleeing for the hills. It was through these dark times that a secret society grew within Sicily in order to unite the native peoples against the invading Arabs and, eventually, the Normans.

This society was named "Mafia" (after the Arabic word for refuge) and over many years – having established itself as a group with its foundations based on family values and heritage – began to transform itself into something with more sinister motivations and intent. In the mid-1920s when Mussolini (1883–1945) set out his intention to rid Sicily of the Mafia, many fled to the United States to escape arrest, where small but growing bands of Italians had already settled – with strong political connections and huge aspirations. Gangs had become a part of American culture and had the ability to infiltrate all levels of society, with the capability of committing more "organized", well-planned, complicated and well-executed crimes than any individual criminal could ever have hoped to have achieved on their own.

Gangs had been forming and operating in distinct areas or regions of the US since the 19th century. The first immigrant gangs to arrive were the Irish, followed by the Italians and then the Jewish community. The Chinese also emigrated to America following hardship and an unstable economic climate in their homeland. There were also gangs that sprang up in the US in retaliation at the immigrant organizations. Ethnic gangs had arrived, but they weren't just confined to the United States. South America had a strong gang culture with drug cartels – particularly in Columbia and then Mexico – who mainly dealt in drug trafficking and extortion. In more recent times, there has been a great deal of violence between rival gangs in Latin America, as the drug routes out of the countries involved became more and more tightly regulated and monitored, and options for trafficking became more limited. Gangs had also arrived in Britain and other European countries and, although the US, Sicily and Latin America each had different criminal cultures, the underworld was spreading in a new and much more organized way across the world. The intent was undoubtedly the same, however: fame, notoriety and money, with the emphasis on wealth and power.

Many criminals are "ordinary" people with families, friends and the same hassles that life throws at those who don't follow a life of crime. Today, there is no definitive explanation on what constitutes a gang, how a gang is formed and why its members are chosen, or why people agree to become part of an organized-crime operation. But it was very different at the beginning of the 20th century. On the streets of London, people passed by seemingly ordinary men – including seamen, labourers, butchers in striped aprons, men in top hats and men-about-town in boaters – and would not have given them a second look but, in actual fact, a large number of them were police officers and detectives working undercover in order to combat the growing organized crime that was sweeping the city.

These police officers had no patrol cars, no 999 system, no forensics teams, no information room at Scotland Yard capable of linking law forces and well-resourced agencies. As policemen at this time "pounded" the streets, many had to dress in disguise in order to remain unsuspected by London's criminals. They were watching out for the vast gangs of pickpockets who controlled the streets; the sly and vicious kidnappers who lurked in wait for unaccompanied children; and the shop-breakers and burglars who were rife in the city. They were also looking for confidence tricksters. There were officers disguised as railway guards, who kept watch for luggage snatchers; and others working as "butchers", who kept an eye out at the markets for those stealing what amounted to many tons of meat every day.

One "butcher" who worked undercover in 1905 was Sergeant Charles Hearn, who became a key witness in a famous murder trial 22 years later. Hearn found an empty cartridge case in a car in Brixton. The clue helped to convict Frederick Browne and William Kennedy of the murder of Constable Gutteridge. Another undercover police officer was John Gillian, who later went on to become chief inspector of Scotland Yard. He investigated the mysterious disappearance of Elsie Cameron in 1924, where his inquiries took him to a poultry farm in Crowborough, Sussex, where the girl's body was found buried under a chicken run. The owner of the farm, Norman Thorne, was the young woman's lover. He was arrested, found guilty of murder and hanged.

In 1905, London's police force consisted of 16,846 men, just 277 less than it boasted in 1959. Practically every police officer worked on the street – it was the only way to get a true look at the crimes being committed – but fingerprint evidence was beginning to come into play. In March 1905 Scotland Yard investigated the brutal murders of Thomas Farrow and his wife, whose battered bodies were found in their paint shop in Deptford, south London. Farrow was robbed of his cash, which had been held in a small cash box. Two brothers, Alfred and Albert Stratton, were brought to justice when Alfred's thumbprint was found to match prints found on the cash box. The brothers died side by side on the scaffold.

However, in the early 1900s, science rarely played a part in helping the police catch criminals and it was the hard, routine work of the officers in disguise, or undercover, that brought Britain's criminals to trial. The routine methods worked at the time: in 1905 more than 125,000 suspects were arrested. By the mid-20th century, many of those arrested were children and, in 1958, no fewer than 51,779 youngsters between the ages of eight and 17 were convicted. Also in 1905, international thieves and crooks began to arrive in London and police officers were sent back to "school" in order to learn French, German, Italian and Yiddish. Motoring offences began to occupy police officers that same year, as speeding and other road charges became commonplace. But 1905 also brought a heatwave, which was accompanied by a crimewave. At the time, the crimewave was attributed to the scorching-hot weather, but far more likely was the infiltration of immigrants to Britain and the increase in the rise of gangs as they retaliated against those stealing "from their own".

In the roaring twenties, you didn't have to be Italian to be part of gangland culture. The ability of the Mafia to beat Prohibition with smuggled whisky and bathtub booze gave gangsters an adventurous air that has never left them. It was also invaluable in catering to the public's needs. Over a period of 50 years, between the 1920s and the 1970s, eight major gang wars thinned the Mafia's ranks but, just prior to this in 1917, the Mafia took on a rival secret society, the Camorra, which had its origins in Naples. The prize was control of the lucrative New York rackets. On 7th September 1917, Mafia boss Nicholas Morella and a bodyguard were lured to a "peace" meeting on Coney Island, where a five-man Camorra hit squad cut them down. The more disciplined Mafia hit back and, 22 deaths later, they took control of New York's underworld. An even bloodier feud followed in Chicago in the 1920s.

The modern Mafia had actually begun with the ending of feudal privileges in Sicily during the 19th century. However, in the 1930s and 1940s, the Mafia built up political power and gained a large degree of control over Italy's largest single party, the Christian Democrats. At the same time, they built up connections in business, the professions, the Church and local government, permeating every facet of Sicilian life. Many left-wing politicians were killed by the Mafia, as were many traditional bandits on the island (it is said that Mafiosi arranged the killing of the then celebrated Sicilian bandit Salvatore Giuliano). There had often been a two-way traffic between Sicily and the United States. Sicilians joined the ranks of American gangs, and those returning from the States to their homeland often brought fresh ideas in profitable crime, particularly with regard to drugs. For nine years, up to 1972, a report had been promised on the extent of the Mafia involvement in Sicily's national and regional politics. Each year that passed, the report failed to appear while the grip on Sicilian life continued unabated. Many Sicilians were cynical about the possibility of surviving, let alone succeeding, if they did not have patronage of powerful friends. "Without Saints, one cannot enter heaven" ran the Sicilian proverb.

Meanwhile, back in New York, Dion O'Banion – an Irishman famed for his sweet tenor voice and the ability to commit murder with a smile – ruled the northeast, where Bugs Moran was one of the mobsters. The south side was ruled by the "Terrible Gennas", six churchgoing Sicilian brothers who specialized in extortion with bombs and bullets. The other contenders were a Polish gang on the southwest side, who earned the respect of their rivals by introducing the tommy gun. Chicago, at the time, was ruled by Jim Colosimo, the boss of the wide-open Levee red-light district. When O'Banion was murdered by John Torrio – an associate of Al Capone – on 10th November 1924, it set off an underworld battle that claimed 500 lives. Torrio also killed Colosimo and took over the Chicago area, but gave it up to Capone two months later after barely surviving an attempt on his life. Capone wasn't even a member of the Mafia at the time – and he had to contend with Bugs Moran.

New York, meanwhile, had been engaged in a gang war among Sicilian factions, which included the likes of Vito Genovese, Albert Anastasia, Joe Bonanno and Lucky Luciano. Lucky betrayed his own leader, Joe Masseria, who was hit with 20 bullets as he played cards in a deserted restaurant on Coney Island. Lucky was impatient at the old-fashioned methods of veteran Mafiosos, who were contemptuously known as "Moustache Petes". He organized the execution of Don Salvatore Maranzano, who had set himself up as the "boss of bosses". In a bloody coup in 1931, known as "The night of the Sicilian Vespers", 40 confederates of Maranzano were executed across America. By 1945, Frank Costello had taken New York and, in 1969, it was the turn of real-life "Godfather" Carlo Gambino. In the 1970s there were rumours that the Mafia was "struggling for its life" as non-Italian and Sicilian gangs scrambled for an increased share of the action. Black gangsters in Harlem were particularly intent on pushing out the Mafia, while Puerto Rican, Cuban and Mexican-American gangs began to become increasingly violent. And, in 1972, a non-Mafia figure became the most powerful influence in international crime. His name was Meyer Lansky, a Russian-born Jew who controlled an empire that enveloped many Mafia groups.

Although ethnic gangs do still exist, the way crime operates in both the US and the UK is radically different to the way in which crime was carried out during Prohibition in the States, for example, and by the likes of Bonnie and Clyde in the early to mid-1930s during the Great Depression. The types of commodities involved are often new and possibly unexpected. Drugs, money laundering, alcohol and cigarettes were big business. Smash and grabs were the order of the day, as was holding-up a small shop or store with a handgun. While drugs and money laundering may still play an important part of gang culture, newer crimes – such as people trafficking and smuggling, kidnap and ransom, fake alcohol and prescription drugs, "hot" metals, the killing of animals for their "medicinal" purposes, animal smuggling and identity theft – are definitely on the increase. Smash and grabs also still exist, but crimes committed by more than one individual are likely to be carried out by a well-informed, organized, knowledgeable gang with the resources and backing to pull off bigger and more complicated crimes. The police and law agencies endeavour to keep up, and bring to justice those perpetrating crime by the use of more and more advanced technology and clever infiltration systems. In the end, however, the only ones really likely to know exactly what's going on within the criminal underworld are those who are part of, and remain loyal and committed to, the gang in which they work and its ever evolving criminal activities.

Individuals

Al Capone

Al Capone's image as the great tsar of American crime – and how he was tamed by clean-cut agents such as Eliot Ness – is mangled by myths, no doubt fostered by countless films and TV shows. Crime writer Carl Sifakis detonated the myths in one of his books on Capone when he revealed that Capone's reputation as an all-powerful crime overlord was unjustified outside Chicago: in fact, he was "small beer" compared to his contemporaries Meyer Lansky and Lucky Luciano and the bloody Mafia empire they created. The notorious nickname, Scarface, that Capone loved, was founded on a lie. Capone had claimed that he got the name fighting in France during the First World War, but in actual fact he was slashed by a hoodlum in a scrap over a girl. And, Eliot Ness wasn't the man who terrified Capone – that honour went to taxman Frank J Wilson, who eventually jailed the crime boss. Also untrue were the rumours that Capone had the ability to terrorize fellow hoodlums and bribe officials in Alcatraz. He was actually ridiculed and attacked, and was known as "The Wop with the Mop" after being made to clean the prison washroom. Despite the name Capone being synonymous with "Chicago gangster", there were many more men who did far more to foster organized crime in America. According to those who have researched Capone, he was just a jumped-up former brothel bouncer who ended his days gibbering from madness brought on by syphilis.

Alphonse Capone was born in Brooklyn, New York in 1899 to Italian immigrants from Naples. He joined the notorious teenage James Street Gang with his friend Johnny Torrio, who later hired Capone as a bouncer at a Brooklyn brothel. He moved to Chicago where he and Torrio arranged the murder of Big Jim Colosimo, recruited hoodlums from New York and took over the dead man's empire. But Torrio was shot in an ambush and decided to get out of the criminal underworld. He basically handed Chicago to Capone. At the age of 26, Capone had become the city's crime boss. The ruthless murderer changed his public image: he mixed with politicians, business people and social figures – and limited his mob's activities to booze, gambling and prostitution. His maniacal rages, though, continued unabated and, when three of his henchmen plotted against him, he invited them to a banquet and then beat their brains out with a club.

But, on 14th February 1929, he blundered when he ordered the St Valentine's Day massacre. Seven men were lined up against a garage wall and machine-gunned to death by Capone's hit men. The real target, arch-enemy Bugs Moran, wasn't even there at the time. The killings outraged even the shock-resistant citizens of Chicago and the government put on pressure for Capone to be tamed. Eliot Ness had formed The Untouchables in 1928 and recruited nine agents, all in their 20s with impeccable records.

Their brief was to smash Capone's mob – whereby the clamour for success became much greater after the massacre. Ness thrived on personal publicity and told the press whenever a major raid was going to take place. This caused an army of photographers to descend in the right place at the right time and, of course, many of the raids were then bungled. However, it was the taxman Frank J Wilson whose name could reduce Capone to "jelly". Wilson put so much heat on Capone that the gangster ordered five gunmen to "get" the man. This was then called off on the advice of Johnny Torrio. Capone fought his last battle in court – where his rivals were armed with ledgers, bookkeepers and accountants – and he was jailed for 11 years for tax evasion. The man who boasted he could buy any official he chose had been beaten. Wilson went on to head the US Secret Service in 1936, while Ness ended his career as federal director, charged with cracking down on venereal disease amongst servicemen.

Capone may not have been the man that everyone came to believe he was, but for the length of his "career" he was feared by many. On Sunday, 13th October 1930, the famous gangster Jack Diamond was shot in a hotel in New York and was taken to the Polyclinic Hospital, where he fought for his life against slim hopes of success. The police ordered the wholesale detention of gangsters known to have associated with Diamond who, before sinking into a coma, told police that two men whom he did not know had fired the shots. Police Commissioner Mulrooney characterized the words as an obvious lie and the hospital was heavily guarded, for fear that the gangsters would return to finish off Diamond. In the meantime, police detained a Ziegfeld showgirl, Marion Roberts (also known as Straswick), who had admitted that she had shared breakfast with Diamond in her room at the Monticolli Hotel. Roberts asserted that she was filling her bath when two men entered her room. She alleged that she heard Diamond pleading for mercy and that shouts followed. The showgirl then fled and hid in a friend's room. She denied that she knew the identity of Diamond's assailants, but said that they came from New Jersey. The attackers' car was said to have had New Jersey licence plates and the police believed that they were liquor runners who objected to Diamond encroaching on their territory. Police had managed to detain three suspects and were said to be searching for hotel manager Jacob Ginsberg, who had carried Diamond to his own room following the shooting. A report came through that the shooting was carried out on the orders of Al Capone, who was alleged to have feared that Diamond was about to reveal his secrets. A raid was made on the home of Scarface in the suburb of Cicero, but didn't turn up anything. It was thought that the gangster had fled by the time the raiders arrived, although 19 men and one woman were arrested. Jack "Legs" Diamond survived that particular attack on his life, but was caught out by other gangsters in 1931.

Earlier in 1930, Al Capone was described as "public enemy number one" as he was hustled by the Chicago police into court on Thursday, 26th February to face a charge of contempt of court. He was guarded more closely than a member of the royal family as he was led into the federal building, which itself was held in a virtual stage of siege with special guards posted all around it. Members of the Capone gang, fearful that the gangster's enemies might try to ambush him, occupied strategic positions all along the route their boss was to take. However, Scarface arrived safely and pleaded not guilty to the charge of contempt. During the lunchtime break, he surrendered himself to the city police who wanted him on a charge of vagrancy. Amid scenes of commotion he was hustled by the police out of the building and taken to the police court, where he was granted bail on the vagrancy charge. He was then rushed back to the federal court in time for the proceedings on the charge of contempt following the lunch break.

Capone's appearances were the first time he had come into the open since the murder of crime reporter Jake Lingle in June 1930, a crime that had started a campaign against the gangsters and a list of "public enemies" drawn up with Capone's name in pride of place at the top. Meanwhile, Judge John H Lyle was baying for the gangster's blood. The ordeal in the federal court brought about an intimation from Capone that he would step down as leader of Chicago's underworld as he said: "I am sick and tired of being made the goat of every politician and reformer." But police believed that his multiple connections with gangland exploits would make his retirement difficult. Two days after the court hearing, Capone was found guilty of contempt and sentenced to six months' imprisonment. It was the first time in 10 years, despite being one of the leading figures in gangland Chicago, that he had been convicted in a local court. He blushed when he heard the sentence, but was able to leave the court when his £1,000 bail was continued and he was granted a stay of sentence.

In October 1931, the tsar of the underworld gave a broad grin when he heard his conviction on five of 23 counts of tax evasion. It was the final day of trial and Capone, looking smart in a light-green suit, waited while the jury deliberated for eight hours before reaching a verdict. With a possible maximum penalty of 17 years, and facing a £12,000 fine, he then walked free from court as, after much discussion, Judge Wilkerson adjourned the court without passing sentence. The judge wasn't happy about the motion and a hearing was fixed for the following week, where the defence promised to cite "a long line of cases". Capone left the court with an even wider grin on his face. But the smug look was gone on Friday, 23rd October 1931 when he was handed an 11-year sentence for being found guilty of income-tax evasion. He looked stunned as the judge also fined him £10,000. It was a ruling that would mark the end of gang power in Chicago, while Capone's total liabilities in connection with the trial were estimated to have amounted to around £50,000. He was given until Tuesday, 27th October to appeal, but no bail was granted. He had spent the previous weekend locked in Cook County Jail, but was now bound for Fort Leavenworth Prison to begin his sentence. The gangland leader, thought responsible for scores of murders, walked up to his attorneys and shook them by the hand saying, "I guess it's all over", as he realized that an application for a writ of "supersedeas" had been denied and he was going back to a cell. As he was led from the courtroom, the dazed and crestfallen gangster was handed a demand for taxes that he had avoided paying, and was then handed a lien on his £8,000 estate in Florida and his safe-deposit boxes in Chicago banks. Livid with rage, Capone appeared to lunge at the deputy collector of internal revenue, but he was quickly restrained by two court marshalls.

Capone ended up in the prison on Alcatraz, in San Francisco Bay, but was moved in July 1936 to McNeil Island, in Washington state, due to the repeated attacks he suffered at the hands of fellow prisoners. He was stabbed with a pair of scissors just two weeks before he was moved. The attacks, it was rumoured, came because Capone had "squealed" on other gangsters and refused to join a mutiny at Alcatraz. Two years later, Capone was back in Alcatraz – America's most terrifying jail at the time – and, in February 1938, there were reports that the one-time king of Chicago gangsters was going mad. His insanity – according to newspaper reports – was caused by terror. He was afraid that fellow convicts who had sworn to "bump him off" would mercilessly snuff out "his miserable life" at any moment. He lost control on 8th February when, screaming and spitting, he attacked "lifers" with his fists and feet, but before the prisoners could strike him down, he was restrained by prison guards. He was taken to the prison's hospital, where he was immediately surrounded by specialists in mental health. Doctors believed that Capone was suffering from paresis, an incomplete form of paralysis, which meant that he had literally become paralysed by fear. It was thought that the authorities would then move him from Alcatraz to an unnamed prison in the east of the United States, where he might have a chance of recovery without fearing other prisoners. But the newspapers warned that any move would have to take place in utmost secrecy in order to avoid rescue attempts by Scarface's old gang members.

The authorities had tried to keep the news of Capone's state confined to prison walls, but inmates who were released had been happy to leak the news of the gang leader's demise. Then, Mae Capone, the boss's faithful wife, made a plea that he should be released so that he could go into a nursing home, where she fully intended to look after him. For much of his time in prison, Capone had been a squealer. He had ratted to wardens about breaches of prison rules in order to gain favour with those in authority. But, in so doing, he put his life in danger on a daily basis. After he was stabbed, a conspiracy to kill the gangster was uncovered – just before it was too late – and he subsequently lived in terror. It was a terror that had turned to eccentricity and was hurtling towards madness. He refused to participate in meals and insisted on wearing Sunday uniform on weekdays. He spent hours dressing and undressing and unmaking his newly made bed. After doctors examined Capone, he was ordered to stay in bed.

On 16th November 1939, Capone, an invalid frightened out of his wits, was met by his relatives at the gates of Lewisburg Prison, Pennsylvania, a free man. He was free, but greatly changed. He was barely recognized by his waiting friends, who witnessed a completely bald, partly paralysed man who stumbled forward to meet them. He had served almost seven years of his 11-year sentence. Just four days before, he had been specially disguised by make-up experts in Alcatraz before being surrounded by guards and taken to a railway station under machine-gun armed guards en route for Lewisburg. Once free, Capone was whisked away to Baltimore Hospital for treatment and observation. He was then expected to go to his luxury mansion in Florida with a host of gunmen who would protect him. But, in effect, Capone wasn't a free man. Gangsters, relatives and friends of the men his gang had shot down had not forgotten the battles of the liquor days and had sworn that they would "get him". Meanwhile, in Chicago, his associates were aiming to make the city safe for him to return and had begun a campaign threatening to "wipe out" any enemies that stood in their way. The Capone gang had decided to fight without a leader after it became clear that seven years in jail had changed the swaggering Italian-American.

The once hard man had learned to become a shoemaker and tailor during his time in prison and his soft white hands had become hard and tough. He had almost been a model prisoner. He had suffered a lonely horror in Alcatraz and his mind had given in – so newspapers reported. He had been found spending hours making and unmaking then remaking his bed. Sometimes he had burst into Italian song. In Florida, Mae and the couple's son Tony waited for his return. Capone's wife, once a flashy blonde, had become a "fat" devout Roman Catholic with grey hair. Their son, popular at Yale University, was good at sport and it was hoped that, unlike his father, he would move in the right circles. Capone was estimated to have made £1.4 million from his gang rackets. However, as a broken, bald old man, it was thought that he would probably say (despite a fortune in the bank) that crime didn't pay.

At the beginning of June 1942, Capone returned to Chicago for the first time since he was sent to prison. But he was haunted by memories throughout his visit and then travelled to Minnesota, where he was known to have taken ill. For months he had tried to persuade Mae to take him back to his former gangland territory so that he could look at the scene of his past glories as a top racketeer. Eventually Mae Capone had given in, but when the couple arrived and called on former friends most of them were fearful and had begged the couple to leave. Capone then made visits to a number of clubs, but found many of the clientele upset by his arrival and then promptly left. At 3.00am in the early hours of one Saturday morning, Capone was seen crying at a table in a club. He died on 25th January 1947 from cardiac arrest following a stroke.

Freddie Foreman

Dubbed the godfather of the Costa del Crime, Freddie Foreman was flown back to Britain on 28th July 1989 in handcuffs. He didn't come quietly. When Spanish police picked him up in a swoop on his apartment in Marbella, newspaper reports claimed that he screamed abuse all the way to the airport. As he stepped off the Iberia Airways jet at Heathrow, a senior Flying Squad officer greeted him with the words: "Welcome back, Freddie." The then 58-year-old former enforcer for the Kray gang was wanted in connection with the £6 million Security Express robbery in London in 1983. He was the first big-name fugitive to be booted out of the Costa del Sol under a ruling by the Spanish Supreme Court earlier in the month.

Flying Squad detectives were waiting on the tarmac at Heathrow as Foreman stepped from the plane, still handcuffed to his Spanish police escort. He looked tanned and fit, dressed in shorts and a T-shirt with sunglasses dangling from a chain around his neck. He was more appropriately attired for the beach than the nick. He was quickly cuffed to a Scotland Yard uniformed officer and driven off for questioning at Leman Street police station. It was a world away from the plush apartment in trendy Marbella that he shared with his wife Maureen.

Foreman's return to the UK sent shudders through the criminal community in the Costa del Sol, which up to that point had been a safe haven. Now, for the underworld, there was a real fear that the

Spanish authorities would expel further exiles in their country. All faced expulsion unless they chose to leave their bolt-holes of their own volition. Amongst those still "hiding out" in Spain was Ronnie Knight (the former husband of actress Barbara Windsor), who was also wanted in connection with the Security Express raid six years previously. Knight, Clifford Saxe and at least a dozen other Britons were fighting expulsion orders through the Spanish courts. However, a senior Spanish official said: "The Supreme Court ruling is a clear message to them that it's time to start packing."

Foreman was finally nailed for his part in the Security Express raid at the Old Bailey on 4th April 1990. He was cleared of taking part in the raid itself but convicted of dishonestly handling £363,000 from the huge haul. The money he handled, it was believed, had been used to set up a drugs empire from his refuge in Spain. The verdicts came seven years to the day after a gang poured petrol over a guard and forced him to hand over keys to the strongroom at the Security Express headquarters in Shoreditch, east London. It left the former gangster's dream of underworld power in tatters. Foreman had once been known as gangland's "undertaker", a hard man who had got rid of Jack "The Hat" McVitie's body after Ronnie and Reggie Kray ordered his killing. By the time he was convicted, Foreman was grey and balding, with a faded tan that had all but disappeared during the eight months he had spent in jail awaiting trial.

Foreman earned his "Mean Machine" nickname as the bully-boy enforcer for the Kray gang, through which he was linked to six killings but was never found guilty of murder. He had previously been jailed for 10 years for his part in the McVitie killing. He was later cleared of the gangland murder of Ginger Marks.

Soon after the Security Express raid, Foreman fled to Spain in a private plane to rule as cockney godfather of the ageing villains sunning themselves in exile. He bought three apartments and a villa. He owned white Rolls-Royces and white silk suits. And, while he and his wife lived in a plush apartment, Foreman ran his own nightclub in Marbella, the Eagles Country Club.

Before the robbery, Foreman and his wife had only £72 in the bank. On the day of the raid, he had applied to have his rent cut to £7 a week by London's Southwark Council. But, within months, he'd banked more than £363,000. Detectives believed that after he fled, he masterminded a multi-million-pound drug-smuggling racket from Spain. After his arrest, he boasted to Spanish police that he had taken part in the robbery, the court heard. He said he was helped by Costa fugitive Ronnie Knight, 55. His counsel, John Mathew, QC, asked the judge to bear in mind when passing sentence that Foreman's wife was seriously ill. It was suspected that Foreman had spent much of his fortune on medical bills for his wife's condition. Mathew stated: "He feels a substantial sentence means that he might not see his wife again."

Meanwhile, detectives wanted to question Foreman's 32-year-old son Jamie who was said, during the trial, to have helped to shift some of the money. Actor Jamie, who was appearing in the hit ITV series *London's Burning* at the time, had allegedly deposited

£50,000 in a London bank soon after the raid. After the trial Detective Inspector Reed McGeorge said: "We would dearly like to speak to him." It was believed that Jamie was in Spain.

In March 2000, Freddie Foreman was arrested after claiming on TV that he was involved in two gangland murders. He was arrested on suspicion of perjury and perverting the course of justice after appearances on two Carlton Television documentaries. He had already been tried and cleared of murdering Frank Mitchell and Tommy "Ginger" Marks. Then, in July that year, actor Jamie Foreman spoke to the press about his gangland father, describing how he loved to listen to classical music and read Shakespeare. He added: "My father and I have got an extraordinary relationship. Friends say the things I've done with my dad, they wouldn't have dreamt of doing with theirs.

"One of my earliest memories is of when we lived above a pub. He'd come up from the bar about 8.30, nine o'clock and tuck me in. He used to wear handmade suits, I could smell his aftershave and the brandy on his breath, and I could feel his weight and his size as he cuddled me. I felt exceptionally safe when he was there." He continued: "He couldn't beat us, ever. It's a bit of a contradiction with his other life, I know." He described how going to see his father in prison for his part in the killing of "The Hat" was unusual. "When you went to see him in jail, he'd stand and hold his arms open and smile. I remember he'd give us money. He'd say: 'There's 50 quid. Now go and see this one, you've got to get a grand off 'im. And that one owes you £1,500'." But, far from wanting his son to follow him into crime, Freddie Foreman was "delighted" when Jamie told his dad he wanted to be an actor.

In 2012, Jamie spoke to newspapers once again about his dad. He told how he was "brought up to be a 'straight goes', live honestly and never take anything that didn't belong [to him]", but that his dad took things that didn't belong to him every day. Foreman junior claimed it was: "just the world I was born into".

Foreman senior had been one of London's most successful gangsters and involved in Britain's most audacious armed robberies with the most dangerous of criminals. However, to his son, he was just "dad". Above the pub where Jamie grew up as a youngster in southeast London, pop stars such as Cat Stevens and Manfred Mann mixed with sporting greats such as Bobby Moore, along with other West Ham, Spurs, Millwall and Chelsea footballers. Other regulars to the haunt were actors and actresses – especially the *Carry On* team – who mixed freely with high court judges and politicians. Foreman's "firm" also met regularly at the pub and the Kray twins would regularly drop by, as would Buster Edwards.

Jamie Foreman was eventually sent to boarding school to protect him from his father's dangerous world. He had always sensed that his dad had "connections" and was linked to something nefarious and secretive. He knew that the visitors to the pub were often strong and dangerous people. His father's connections also brought about the finer things in life during the swinging sixties in London; there were shopping trips to Harrods and holidays to Portugal, Morocco, Jamaica and the Bahamas. When Foreman was serving 10 years for the disposal of "The Hat", his son discovered that he was a gangland killer at the centre of the most powerful crime organization in Britain. Foreman had been part of the longest trial in British criminal history, involving the Krays, who had babysat Jamie Foreman. He had been left at their East End snooker hall as Foreman conducted some "business". Foreman had done some terrible things. For a time, Jamie Foreman blamed the Krays for his dad's actions, but in the end he realized that the man he admired and adored had done the things he'd done by his own volition. No one had made Freddie Foreman a gangster; he had done that for himself.

Frankie Fraser

On 16th June 1967, gangland member Francis "Mad Frankie" Fraser, a leading light in the Charles Richardson torture squad, was given a 10-year jail sentence after being convicted of assault and demanding money with menaces in the "torture" trial that ended at the Old Bailey the previous week. The sentence would start once Fraser had finished serving five years – sentenced in 1966 – for a shooting affray at a club in Catford, south London. His 10-year sentence had been postponed while other charges were considered but, when sentencing was passed, Justice Lawton told Fraser: "After Charles Richardson, you were the most vicious member of the gang." The judge also ordered Fraser to pay costs not exceeding £2,000 and commented: "I am satisfied that during the period immediately before your arrest you acquired ill-gotten gains."

Fraser, who was described as a company director from Hove in Sussex, was said to have had 17 previous convictions and that he had been both in prison and hospitals catering for those with mental health issues. The judge was told how Fraser had earned a living in the years prior to 1966 by taking "protection" money. His nephew, 24-year-old James Fraser from Walworth in south London, pleaded not guilty to demanding money but admitted to assault. Albert Longman, 41, also made similar pleas, which were accepted by the prosecution. The judge ordered that both men –

who had been in custody since the previous July – should be given sentences meaning an immediate discharge. He confirmed that the men had undoubtedly already served the sentence that they would have been given for assault.

On 30th July 1970, Fraser was identified and convicted of being one of the Parkhurst Prison rioters. He was given another five years. "Appeal Frankie, appeal!" cried Fraser's sister Eva at the dock. She was taken from the court while her brother was led away to face the five-year sentence, on top of the 15 he was already serving. The judge, Justice Bean, had described the 46-year-old as a ringleader of the riot in October 1969. He told him: "In civilian life you became a menace to society, and you seem determined to become the same in prison life." The six others found guilty of offences connected with the riot were given sentences ranging from six years to 18 months, in addition to their then current sentences. One by one, they were whisked away from the Isle of Wight to separate top-security jails. Forty other prisoners who gave evidence for the defence were also moved out of Parkhurst and big changes were planned at the jail. The governor, Alaistair Miller, was leaving to become the governor of Pentonville Prison and, in court, the judge called for a probe of Parkhurst's punishment cells.

In May 1985 Fraser, known as "The Axeman" and "The Enforcer", began a new life of freedom after spending 19 years being transferred 106 times around Her Majesty's jails. He was paroled on a Friday afternoon and showed up at Wembley on the

Saturday to cheer for Everton in the FA Cup final. On the Sunday, he was cheering on local cricket team Sussex at Hove in a match against a touring Australian side. But life didn't completely turn out to be a bed of roses for "Mad Frankie" Fraser, who was shot in August 1991 outside a central London club (he was able to leave hospital a few days later). Three years later, actor Bob Hoskins was slammed in the press by former underworld crook John McVicar – once dubbed Public Enemy Number One – for glamorizing Britain's meanest villains in a BBC series, *The Underworld*. In a scathing attack in 1994, the reformed criminal who worked as a broadcaster and journalist stated that: "Hoskins is in awe of these people. It's disgusting the way Hoskins narrates with that reverential tone.

"It's like he's paying homage to these people who were animals. When you talk about the Krays and the Richardsons and killings and the torture, even in underworld terms what they did was a disgrace." McVicar went on to say: "He talks about 'Mad Frankie' Fraser from the Richardson gang with such reverence yet I know a story about Fraser that is horrific.

"One victim of the gang was taken to the Richardsons' scrap yard in south London, nailed under the floorboards by Fraser and made to eat his own excrement with tomato sauce on it. I can't believe the BBC have made such an uncritical programme with Hoskins treating these people like Gods." A spokeswoman for Hoskins, Liz Soussi, refuted McVicar's charges saying: "Bob has pitched his voice low for effect." And, the producer of the programme, Lorraine Heggessey said: "Bob's voice is meant to be chilling, not reverential."

In an interview in 1995, the former gangland enforcer described how he didn't really like being known as "Mad", but said: "I've only got myself to blame." In a meeting for the *Mirror*, the interviewer said: "Sitting next to this small, endlessly polite old man who smiles and laughs a lot it is very hard to imagine him wielding a hatchet, brandishing a gun or pulling out teeth." Fraser himself stated: "I got myself into Broadmoor the first time by pretending to be mad. A mate had told me it was easier in there than prison and he was right, although it was dead boring. The other two times I was sent there because they didn't know what to do with me. But, they knew I wasn't mad."

Fraser used the title *Mad Frank* for his book, so it couldn't have bothered him too much. But one thing that did bother him was the fact that he was accused of pulling out teeth with pliers. He said it never happened. Yet, he was happy to admit to "lots of violence, there was lots of violence", and admitted that he was hurt on a number of occasions. He was asked in the interview if he'd ever committed murder – he was never accused of murder – and he said: "I dare say there were a couple." He also admitted that he missed his old life, but he didn't miss prison. He'd received the birch, the cat and had been beaten from pillar to post; following the Parkhurst riots he had found himself in a wheelchair for six weeks. He told how he'd had every rib broken several times, had been on hunger strike for weeks, and had been subjected to more solitary than any man alive. During the interview, Fraser spoke with some regret about how, during the 20 years he served for his role as gang boss Charlie Richardson's enforcer, he attacked nine prison governors. However, it wasn't the violence he regretted, it was the fact he hadn't made the number into double figures. By 1995 Fraser was in a relationship with Marilyn Wisbey, the daughter of one of the Great Train Robbers, who managed to tame him. He reckoned he could have been Britain's most violent man at one time, but he wasn't sure and had no intention of ever going back inside. However, not being a gambling man, he would not put money on it. At the time of the interview in January 1995 he was due to speak at Wesley's Chapel, London, the world's top Methodist Church, where other speakers had included the likes of Cardinal Basil Hume. He was to tell the audience what his life had been like and to answer questions. Asked if he was nervous, the reply came: "I'm not nervous. Well, no more than if I was going out on a bank job."

In 1996, he advertised himself and his availability in *The Stage*, the actors' newspaper, to publicize that he was keen on a life in showbiz. The ad read: "Retired gangster Mad Frankie Fraser is available for pantomime". In January 1997, Fraser was doing business in London's Groucho club – an exclusive haunt for actors, producers and other celebrities – when he was approached by Liam Gallagher and his then muse, Patsy Kensit. Asked by Gallagher what he was doing, Fraser said: "Do you know who I am, son?" "Course I do!" came the reply. Fraser then said: "So who are you?" There was an uneasy silence. The Mancunian musician shifted and met the dead, pitiless eyes head on. But, the 73-year-old gangster then laughed and stuck out his hand. It seems that apart from cockney ex-mobsters with holes in their gums, everyone was mad for Frankie Fraser. For, at this point, Fraser had become the world's first stand-up gangster comedian.

It was a far cry from the former 1960s henchman who had a reputation for killing, torturing, trying to hang a prison governor and who had spent 40 years in jail with one day's remission. Known for decades as Britain's most violent man, Fraser had a show that was in the middle of a West End run and looked to be taking it on a national tour. During the show he told tales about how he'd had no option but to take out screws and grasses. On stage, belting out the songs for the act, was his partner Marilyn Wisbey. It was also rumoured that Fugitive Films wanted to make a movie about him, with the actor Martin Kemp in the lead. Ironically, the probable leading lady was to be Patsy Kensit. Fraser thought Kensit was "terrific", but had a slight problem with her playing the part as, if things had turned out differently, he might have killed her father.

Jimmy Kensit was a grass who met Fraser in 1960. Fraser said: "He was quite a nice fella, but even then there were whispers about him. He got nicked with me in 1966 and was suddenly transferred to Lewes Prison. Then he was let go. He'd made a statement. He'd grassed." He continued: "I hate grasses.

It's quite possible I could have killed him. But I'd never take it out on his daughter. You can't, can you? Sins of the father and all that." Fraser had killed before. "They never did me for murder, but I did kill. I won't say how many times. And I was happy to do it, because when I did, he was getting what he deserved. It was kill or be killed. We all knew what game we were in." But Fraser claimed he wouldn't have changed a thing, otherwise he wouldn't have become who he was. What made Frankie different from most ex-gangland criminals who go public was that he had no remorse and offered no defence. He knows he was a villain, and knew by the late 1990s that he was a celebrity villain; he simply told it like it was.

Fraser had been born into poverty in London's Elephant and Castle on 19th November 1923, one of six children. His mother was Irish, his father half American-Indian, which explained Fraser's complexion and dark eyes. By the age of eight he was involved in crime. At 13, he was in borstal. At 17, he got 18 lashes of the birch for "taking out a warder" and that, Fraser claimed, was the turning point. Institutions had made him violent. He was just 17 years old when the 18 lashes were dished out, followed by 14 nights in solitary with no mattress and only bread and water. It was brutal. At age 13 he'd had a fight that had lasted all day, then being in an institution took violence to a whole new level and he suffered because he "wouldn't take any crap". After nine assaults on governors – usually by putting urine pots over their heads and cracking them on the skull – he led the Parkhurst riot before taking on Governor W J Lawton. He ambushed the man as he walked his dog on Wandsworth Common, but Lawton escaped death because the branch that Fraser tried to hang him from snapped. The dog wasn't that lucky.

As for attacks on prison wardens, Fraser lost count. In later life, with his smart dress sense, cufflinks and gold watch, the only thing that gave him away was a scar on his forehead where a bullet hit him as he left a pub. He liked the then prime minister Tony Blair's words about being tough on the causes of crime. Poverty caused thieving, which is why Fraser had got into robbing. He did it for his family. But he was adamant that no youngsters in modern Britain would want to follow his example. He'd been inside for 40 years – possibly one of the most unsuccessful thieves ever – and most of those had been spent in solitary.

In June 1997 Fraser went to court to champion Charlie Kray, the elder brother of Ronnie and Reggie. He told the court that Kray was a lovely man, and that regarding the charge against him of masterminding a £39 million cocaine-smuggling plot they had the wrong man. Fraser gave evidence that Charlie Kray was "the last person" who should be in the dock: he had always run at the first sign of trouble, wasn't a bit like his brothers and did not advocate drugs. He told how he'd become very friendly with Ronnie and Reggie and had got to know the older Kray well, and that there was no way that he could have become involved in drugs. The Krays and the Richardsons, according to Fraser, didn't agree with drugs. Charlie Kray didn't believe in crime. In Fraser's words, the older Kray brother – although a lovely man – had been a nobody.

Drugs and drug smuggling did, however, feature in Fraser's life when his grandson, Anthony, was being hunted by police in February 2011 and his face was due to be unveiled in Alicante on 21st February by *Crimestoppers*. Two years earlier, £5 million worth of cannabis was found at a storage unit in Grays, Essex. Five people were jailed, but Anthony who was suspected of involvement was alleged to have gone on the run.

Today, Fraser is a TV celebrity and offers gangland tours around London.

Jimmy Hoffa

In September 1958 James "Jimmy" Hoffa was attacked in a "naming and shaming exercise" by Senator John McClellan, chairman of the Senate Committee (responsible for stamping out gangland activities), as being a "menace" to the United States. Hoffa, the boss of America's biggest trades union and head of the Teamsters' (lorry drivers') Union, was described as a source of a "cancer" that had spread corruption and violence in the union. It was claimed that union funds amounting to £2.5 million had been mishandled, lent to gangsters and invested in projects backed by Hoffa's friends. There were calls for Hoffa's immediate resignation or removal, when McClellan described him as seeking power greater than that of the government. He "has not only placed hoodlums in key positions in the union," said the senator, "but he and his chief lieutenants have consorted with the major racketeers in the US". The Senate Committee had been investigating Hoffa's activities for some time and the report of its hearing, published on 21st September 1958, mentioned countless oppressive tactics against members who tried to oust their corrupt leaders.

Hoffa was eventually brought to court in December 1962 for an alleged £350,000 graft conspiracy. However, a gunman burst into the proceedings and shot Hoffa, hitting him in the arm and back as the president of the Teamsters' Union ducked just in time. US marshalls piled into the scrimmage and some of the 60 spectators joined in, beating and kicking the gunman as he lay on the floor. At this point, Hoffa's trial in Nashville, Tennessee, had been in progress for six weeks. It was announced in March 1964 that Hoffa was closer to jail than he had been, but arch-enemy Attorney General Robert Kennedy had still not managed to put him behind bars.

Hoffa had been sentenced to eight years in Chattanooga jail, Tennessee, on charges of trying to "fix" a jury, but he promptly lodged an appeal and had been released on bail. He had been in a "feud" with the 38-year-old younger brother of assassinated President John Kennedy since 1957, when Robert became the lawyer for the Labour Rackets Committee set up by the senate. Kennedy decided that Hoffa, who had given many gangster friends money-spinning posts in the Teamsters, could be the most dangerous man in America. He was eventually given five more years on 17th August 1964 – to be served in Chicago – for his part in defrauding the union of £8.4 million. He was then released on bail pending an appeal. His sentence for bribing two jurors was still under appeal. He was expected to serve eight years in Chattanooga, followed by the sentence in Chicago.

He began his sentence three years later in Tennessee on 7th March 1967, when his lawyers lost a last-ditch effort in Washington Federal Appeals Court to secure a further delay to the start of the sentence. An appeal for his Chicago sentence was still under consideration. It was feared that, with Hoffa in jail, the union would be split by a violent leadership battle, although Hoffa hoped he would still be able to control important decisions from his prison cell.

When Hoffa entered jail, he left behind his marble-palace offices in Washington, the unswerving loyalty of 1.8 million members, the friendship of bunny girls and airline hostesses and, perhaps, some of the tremendous power that he wielded. His "brotherhood" of Teamsters, it was stated, could paralyse America if it went out on strike. As he was taken to jail, Hoffa shouted: "This is the result of a vendetta and if it can happen to me, it can happen to anyone." Police officers were guarding the man responsible for his demise, Robert Kennedy, who had received a number of anonymous phone calls threatening to kill him if Hoffa went to jail.

Blackmail and theft, frequently backed by murder, had flourished for a long time in American trade unions. Congress and responsible union leaders had fought hard against crime, but gangsters still controlled some unions on the docks, building sites and in parts of the clothes and garments industry. Until a few years previously, gangsters had openly dominated the docks. They settled leadership disputes with bullets and collected millions of pounds per year from stolen cargoes. In addition, there was "protection" for shippers and significant funds to be made from moneylending. At this time, death was the penalty of those who dared to break the sinister code on New York's waterfront. The Mafia was still a power in some unions, while its gangsters looted the members' pension funds. Around this time, two officials from a Californian branch of the Painters' Union were murdered when they tried to stop other organized criminals stealing funds.

The bosses of many large haulage firms, it was believed, would be sorry to see Hoffa behind bars. Whatever his tactics, he always kept to agreements and made sure his workers did the same. Despite the fact he was now in jail, he was still worshipped by many of the lorry workers in his union. Hoffa's greed and his support for gangsters had been forgiven because his personality won workers more money, better conditions and shorter working hours. It was believed that members had agreed that Hoffa would still be paid his £35,000 salary while in jail. But, it wasn't the first time that a leader of the Teamsters' had been behind bars. Dave Beck, the man whom Hoffa replaced, was sentenced to two and a half years for tax evasion.

Despite the fact that Hoffa had been sent to jail, nepotism and corruption continued to blight the unions. In September 1969, Tony "Boss" Boyle, received a welter of unsavoury accusations when America's 120,000 coal miners prepared to elect their union president. But only a handful of rebels – led by a former Boyle aid, Joseph Yablonski, and backed by the self-appointed public watchdog Ralph Nader – believed that he could be ousted from office in the December 1969 voting. Boyle had inherited and perpetuated a power structure that guaranteed him almost dictatorial powers over the rank and file of the United Mine Workers of America union. He had an executive board padded with cronies he appointed, and a tight grip on the vast majority of the union's voting branches. He also had the invaluable asset (in American political terms) of a folksy, hard-knuckled style. It was virtually an impregnable defence even against the suggestions of scandal, which never lurked far below the surface in the machinations of many of America's gigantic trade unions. The classic case of Jimmy Hoffa underscored the effectiveness of Boyle's stronghold.

Despite being in jail, Hoffa remained president of the world's largest union, due to the backing of the two-million strong brotherhood of Teamsters with assets of £1 billion. Such was his hold over the membership, both practical and charismatic, that he was re-elected by acclamation and had his pay increased to £42,000 the year after he was convicted. Not one of the Teamsters' 850 local branches had dissented. In 1968, a petition was presented to the US president, Lyndon B Johnson, asking him to "return Mr Hoffa to his members and his family". Hoffa, before he had become unstuck under the relentless pressure of Kennedy, had woven an intricate pattern of power aided by some of the country's highest-paid lawyers. His wife, Josephine Hoffa, remained on the payroll as a high-ranking official with a salary of £18,000 a year. And, behind the union's smooth front, Hoffa couldn't resist a tough-guy response to Kennedy's probing. He once said: "I'd like to break his arm." Boss Boyle wasn't able to resist a similar reaction to the troublesome prodding coming from Ralph Nader and offered to: "meet him in the alley".

The revolt within the United Mine Workers of America (UMWA) presented the first threat to a reigning president for 40 years. Boyle, as the protégé of the much celebrated John L Lewis (who remained a god-like figure to the miners until his death), came to the top in 1963 and was about to bid for his second full term in office. He faced a barrage of accusations about the running of UMWA, which was one of the oldest, possibly the richest and certainly one of the most unchanged unions in the United States. There were claims that the union payroll had been swollen with Boyle's relatives and there were charges of bending the union's charter by preserving the voting rights of branches composed entirely of retired miners on pensions. Yablonski alleged that, since 1959, more than US$1 million had been paid in salaries and expenses to close relatives of Boyle and the union's treasurer, secretary John Owens. The list of salary drawers also included Boyle's lawyer daughter in Montana and his brother Richard, as president of the boss's old union district (also in Montana). Nader, weighing in against the union hierarchy, claimed that there were 400 bogus union branches maintained under Boyle's regime for voting purposes. The power battle sweeping the coalfields promised to provide some of the most bitter union warfare that the United States had seen for many years. Yablonski had been one of Boyle's most sycophantic supporters but changed his mind due to a troubled conscience.

On 23rd December 1971, Jimmy Hoffa was released from jail with more than eight years of his sentence still to be served. He was granted his freedom on the orders of President Nixon, who had been given advice by Attorney-General John Mitchell. Hoffa was ordered not to take part in trade union management. This had all come about when Hoffa entered a "pardon" agreement with the president in order to secure his release. He was banned from taking part in union activities until 1980, which was when his prison sentence would have come to an end.

Hoffa disappeared from outside a restaurant in Detroit on 30th July 1975. He was declared legally dead on 30th July 1982. He was probably the only American trade union leader to become known in Britain prior to the 1970s, partly because he was a buccaneer, partly because he was a millionaire and partly because he was once the head of what was described as "a hoodlum empire". While in prison, Hoffa became quite a mouthpiece on prison reform. He was, according to newspaper reports, a "vivid personality" who (outside of jail) moved in the best of circles and who would probably have taken back his union in 1980 had he been around.

In August 1975, the FBI joined in the search for Hoffa, indicating that the former head of the Teamsters had probably been kidnapped. In fact, an FBI spokesman said that ransom demands had been received. The Teamsters were at the time in a vicious feud with the Mafia and police believed that the former boss was undoubtedly dead. That same month, blood was found on the front seat of a car driven by Hoffa's foster son, Charles O'Brien – who claimed the blood came from salmon – and was tested to see if it was Hoffa's: the car that O'Brien was driving was owned by the son of a Detroit Mafia chief.

A search for Hoffa's body took place in rubbish dumps in New Jersey's swampland in December 1975 while witnesses maintained that he was snatched and murdered by the Mafia. In 1978, it was reported that while it seemed likely that Hoffa had been murdered, no one was likely to be convicted of the crime. His body had never been found and, according to at least one man, they thought it likely that he had probably been fed into a garbage shredder owned by Mafia mobsters. The FBI were stumped because no one was willing to testify in court against the men they suspected of murdering and disposing of Hoffa. One gangster was reported as saying: "Jimmy was ground up in little pieces, shipped to Florida and dumped in a swamp." It was thought that Hoffa, a former friend to the Mafia, made a deal with the devil. However, some staunch unionists believed that Hoffa was the good guy, the one who did more for the Labour movement in America than anyone else. It was usual, they stated, for top bosses to have goons to come in and "bust a few heads". Hoffa was undermined by big businesses and Bobby Kennedy because they didn't like the power he had – at least that's what those who were on his side thought …

Dutch Schultz

Known as the Beer Baron of the Bronx, Dutch Schultz and his lieutenant, Daniel Amacio, were arrested on 18th June 1931. Amacio was shot in the stomach while attempting to escape and was seriously wounded, while Schultz was captured after a chase along five blocks in New York. He was later released on bail for £30,000. Schultz was a New York City Jewish American gangster of the 1920s and 1930s who made a fortune out of organized crime. He participated in activities including bootlegging, but found his rackets threatened by Lucky Luciano – a fellow gangster – following two tax-evasion trials that had severely weakened his finances.

In March 1933, Schultz appeared in Paris after mystifying his gangster friends and the police when he disappeared from his regular haunts in New York. He was being kept under surveillance by the French Secret Service and had been ordered to leave the country; he had a visa for Germany and an arrest was likely if the United States applied for his extradition. He was back in the US in 1935, where he faced a trial for income-tax evasion, but at the proceedings he urged the authorities to economize in order to save taxpayers' money. He went from being Public Enemy Number One to the taxpayers' friend, said newspaper reports. Schultz, whom the Department of Justice had sworn to put in prison beside Al Capone, was shocked to hear that Martin Conboy, district attorney for Southern New York, had resigned his post to conduct the prosecution's case at the trial. The gangster pointed out that Conboy would: "get a nice big fee instead of a flat salary as US District Attorney" and advocated that it was a pretty serious matter since it would mean expenditure of more of the taxpayers' money.

Then, on 24th October 1935, Schultz – described as the last of the "big time" American racketeers – died of bullet wounds in Newark, New Jersey. The gangster, delirious at the end, kept repeating: "It's the journey's end, the journey's end. This is my death. But I won't run." He and a fellow gangster were wounded and two of his bodyguards, Otto Berman and Leo Frank, (along with a bystander) were fatally shot when two gunmen opened fire on Schultz as he ate in a Newark restaurant the day before. Two other members of Schultz's gang had been critically wounded in a barber's shop in New York. The reports read: "Dutch Schultz, cold-blooded beer baron, who terrified even rival gangsters by his sheer nerve, is dead."

Born Arthur Flegenheimer on 6th August 1902, in East Side, New York, Schultz loved to boast that he came from Chicago. He started his criminal career as a hijacker, pirating bootleggers' cargoes in the Peapack country in New Jersey. Al Capone was one of the first of his victims when Schultz shot Blubber Stern, Scarface's lieutenant and right-hand man, on the steps of the Charm Club in New York. From that moment on, he put his thumbs in the armholes of his waistcoat and called himself a tough guy.

Schultz's meeting with a red-haired Irish woman, Red Riordan, was – it was said – one of the worst things to happen to America for many years (and yet the best thing to happen to Schultz). She encouraged Schultz to be "big time" and to get into rackets in New York. Riordan also told him to run his own mob and get his own territory, or, if there wasn't any territory left, to kill off another gang and steal their patch. Schultz did exactly what Red Riordan suggested, and he introduced the fashion of carrying a gun under the arm instead of in the hip pocket. Several gangsters died because they didn't know what Schultz was reaching for inside the breast of his coat. He admitted to killing eight men. He had never been known to "bat an eyelid" in any circumstances and, when he told stories of his killings, he told funny stories alongside describing the murders, lit cigarettes and never changed his facial expression. Red Riordan, undoubtedly the guiding star of his career, received emeralds rather than the usual diamonds given to so many gangsters' molls. And, each time he added a new piece to his growing territory, he added a new emerald to the ring that Riordan wore. Schultz, it was stated: "didn't believe in taking his victims for a ride". He argued that it was better to shoot them where they stood in the middle of the city, where the police had thousands of people to deal with, than in a less populated spot where suspects could be quickly narrowed down; and he slept with dogs in his bedroom, who acted as his bodyguards. The man who killed Schultz was believed to be 21-year-old Albert Stern, brother of Blubber, who had sworn that he would avenge his brother's death and kill the "big time" gangster.

Following Schultz's death, it was discovered that he was

seemingly friendless and alone; his body lay waiting in Potter's Field, the last resting place for down and outs whose relatives were unable to pay for their burials. Yet, Schultz was alleged to have made thousands of dollars a month out of his rackets. Yet, after he died, not one person out of the hundreds of acquaintances who were formerly eager to gain his favour, had come forward to claim his body. On Monday, 28th October 1935, it still lay unclothed, without being embalmed and without a coffin.

By this time, Albert Stern was also dead, said to have taken his own life. He had been found by police hanging in a gas-filled room in extremely shabby clothes in a cheap boarding house where he lived. His landlady confirmed that Stern had had no money and had been unable to pay his rent. He was known to police as a "wild killer" despite his mild-looking appearance and was described as absolutely ruthless in removing anyone who got in his way in the gambling racket. His sworn foe was Dutch Schultz.

While Schultz lay on the slab, the police began a search for another mysterious gangster who was said to aspire to the rank of "Dictator" of New York's underworld. This new man was said to have marked down for death no fewer than 25 rival gang leaders.

But, even more shocking for the residents of New York was the news that, found in the back room of the restaurant in which Schultz and his racketeers were shot down, were papers which alluded to the fact that the former boss had been paying thousands of dollars to certain politicians and police officers for protection in the operation of his rackets. No definite details had been leaked, but hundreds of names and addresses, along with telephone numbers – including those of many women and henchmen – were said to have been found in a number of memorandum books. One of the ledgers found in the back room revealed that Schultz's henchman, Martin Krompier (who was also shot and still in a critical condition at this point), had been earning £300 (approximately £17,500 today) a week.

The latest figure in the case of Schultz was a mysterious woman, identified by the police as "the masked woman". She was described as the only dependable witness able to identify the leader of the assassins, and who had already viewed a number of suspects by the end of October 1935. The woman had seen all the suspects at the Newark police headquarters but had had no success in identifying anyone. On 29th October, Schultz was buried in great secrecy at the gate of Heaven Cemetery in New York. What was puzzling police was how many women he actually had in his life. At least three "Mrs Schultz's" had already been identified.

Schultz's lawyer, Dapper Dixie Davis, a man who bought £50 (worth about £3,000 today) suits and never missed an important concert, could have been one of America's top lawyers. However, he preferred the easy money of the underworld. Davis had fled when Schultz slumped wounded in the restaurant, but was later arrested in the arms of a showgirl, Hope Dare, during the early months of 1938. After his arrest, Davis broke one of the greatest laws of the underworld: he "squealed". The lawyer formally pleaded guilty to the charges brought before him and promised to tell all he knew.

Hope Dare was also to be a key witness after the one-time showgirl became involved with gangsters. It was said that it was Dare who encouraged Davis to squeal, but the couple were in trouble – as gangsters didn't care for those who broke the rules and talked.

In 1941, the guns of Baby-Face Nelson, Al Capone, Dutch Schultz and Baby Killer Coll were said to be on their way to Britain's Home Guard during the Second World War. The Federal Government announced that it was making ready for the shipment of machine guns, tommy guns, sawed-off carbines, pistols and even a few home-made weapons taken from those named and many other gangsters in the preceding years. Many of the weapons were known to have connected with some of the biggest crime stories ever to hit the front pages. The shipment was also to include the machine gun used by Machine Gun Kelly at the St Valentine's Day massacre in Chicago, ordered by Al Capone, when seven men from Bugs Moran's gang were lined up against a garage and shot down. The tommy gun used by Baby Killer Coll, who fired at a rival and missed – killing a child playing in the street – was also bound for British shores. Meanwhile, it came to light that Schultz had been assassinated by The Commission, the governing body of the American Mafia.

Jack Spot

On 11th August 1955, detectives kept a vigil at the hospital bedside of a man who once described himself as "Britain's No 1 Gangster". Jack Comer, known to many as Jack Spot, was found unconscious with stab wounds in his stomach after a struggle on a London street. Hundreds of shoppers saw the attack, which took place on Frith Street, Soho; women screamed and cars jammed on their brakes to avoid the men, both of whom collapsed after about 30 seconds. Police cars cordoned off the street where the victim was found, while detectives discovered a long knife at the scene and ordered that the two men should be sent to different hospitals. In one London hospital, detectives sat by the bedside of a man who had given his name as Albert Dimes. He, too, had severe stab wounds to the stomach.

CID officers from Scotland Yard then searched various gang haunts for men they believed could tell them about the incident. A dozen men who were seen at the scene of the incident had disappeared. Spot had styled himself as Britain's number one gangster in a series of articles he had written for a Sunday newspaper. He claimed to be a cockney kid who fought his way to the head of an "army" of a thousand tough men in London. At one time shortly after the end of the Second World War, he claimed they armed themselves with sub-machine guns, hand grenades and pistols when threatened by a rival gang. But the gang war never came. The gangster claimed that, on his orders, all the weapons were dumped and that gang war in London was brought to an end in 1947. Spot, a bookmaker, claimed to have brought peace to racecourses all over the country by bringing hoodlums under his control and banning violence. The nickname "Spot" came about because Comer always seemed to be "on the spot" when trouble broke out (although some reports alleged it was due to a large mole on his cheek).

On 12th August 1955, two men called to see Jack Spot in hospital in Middlesex, only to find that they were turned away on the grounds that Comer was only well enough to see close relatives and detectives, as ordered by the hospital's medical officer. The two men were then sought by Scotland Yard, who wanted to know who they were and what they wanted with Spot, who lay in great pain in his hospital bed. A nurse who saw the men had told them she would call the matron, but had told the detectives at the victim's bedside instead. Once the detectives reached the hospital gates, however, the two men had disappeared. Their descriptions were given to all officers inquiring into the struggle between Comer and Albert Dimes, who they knew to be Italian Albert, an underworld figure. As Dimes lay seriously ill in Charing Cross Hospital, the police were beginning to piece together the story in which three London gangs were said to be competing for power. One group came from the West End, another from the Aldgate area, while the third gang was said to come from Elephant and Castle. Detectives began mingling with known associates, who were apparently waiting for the order that might have sparked a gang war.

By 22nd August, the self-styled "King of Soho", Spot, sat in court as the story of the knife battle was related. In the same dock at Marlborough Street sat Italian Albert, a bookmaker. There was just one policeman between the two men. Both were charged with possessing a knife and causing each other grievous bodily harm. Both men's defence counsels asked for bail, but this was opposed by the police. The magistrate then remanded both men and agreed to fix a special day for a hearing. On 29th August at Marlborough Street Magistrates Court, the prosecutor Mr E G MacDermott claimed that Spot had started the alleged fight in Soho when he stabbed Albert Dimes. Dimes had then fled into a fruit shop but Comer followed, still attacking, and Dimes managed to wrestle the knife from him. Both men were, again, separated in the dock by a policeman. They were charged separately with wounding with intent to cause grievous bodily harm to each other, and with being in possession of an offensive weapon. They were also charged with fighting and causing an affray.

Dimes had been stabbed in the stomach, thigh and chin and had a 6in wound on his scalp that had required 20 stitches. Jack Spot had fared worse and had wounds in the arm and chest (one blow had penetrated a lung) and his face was slashed. The first witness at the hearing – who, for his own protection, was allowed to write down his name, address and occupation rather than say it out loud – told how Spot had approached Albert and said: "I want to talk to you", and the two men had walked off together.

The witness then stated that, within a short distance, he heard a shout and saw Dimes standing in the road with Spot facing him from the pavement. He then saw Dimes heading for the fruit shop with Spot following. He could see that Spot had a weapon but was unsure whether it was a knife or a dagger. The second witness was also allowed to write down his name and address, although it was known that he worked in the fruit shop. Mr B A Perkoff, acting for Comer, objected to all the secrecy, but it stood in court once it was established that the witness had written down his private address. The second witness had been serving in the fruit shop at about 11.00am when Dimes ran in, bleeding from the chin. He then described how Spot had continued to attack Dimes. Both men were sent for trial at the Old Bailey. Spot was remanded in custody, while Dimes was granted bail of £250 and two sureties of £250.

On 19th September 1955, the trial began at the Old Bailey, with many faces from Soho turning up to follow the proceedings. Both men pleaded not guilty to the charges arising in connection with the stabbings. Witnesses told their stories to the court and some were asked if they knew of any trouble regarding betting-pitch monopolies on racecourses. One of the witnesses was Hyman Hyams, the greengrocer at Continental Fruit Stores at the corner of Frith Street and Old Compton Street, who described how the two men fought in his shop. The trial came to a sudden and sensational end the following day when the judge, Justice Glyn-Jones, directed that the jury should find the men not guilty on certain charges and that both men should be given new and separate trials on the remaining charges. He also ordered that the jury should be dismissed and that a new jury should take its place. He ordered that the jury should not find the men guilty on the affray charge, and withdrew the charge against Dimes of being in possession of an offensive weapon. The jury hadn't been able to reach verdicts on which they could agree and the judge dismissed them.

It transpired that Spot had been warned to keep away from racecourses by Dimes, who worked for the bookmaker Bert Marsh. Spot was convinced that the two men were jealous of him and his "racing" past, which spanned 20 years. But Spot had taken no notice of the warning or the fact that Marsh thought he'd had too many good pitches for far too long, and eventually had received a phone call asking him to meet Dimes in Frith Street. Spot claimed he was then given a final warning by Dimes on behalf of Marsh. On 23rd September 1955 Spot was eventually cleared of the charges against him. The foreman of the jury at the Old Bailey announced that the verdicts of not guilty were unanimous. Spot had claimed that he didn't have the knife and that Dimes was the first to strike.

An elderly clergyman told the court how he saw the struggle between the two men and that the reports in the newspapers were so different from what he'd actually seen that he had come forward as a witness. The Reverend Basil Claude Hudson Andrews told how he had seen Dimes strike first with a weapon. Spot had been defending himself against Dimes, who was still on bail and awaiting his own trial. Dimes was also acquitted at the Old Bailey on both charges when the recorder, Sir Gerald Dodson, said that because of the acquittal of Spot it would be unjust to continue the trial against Dimes.

But, that wasn't an end to the case. A probe into "certain aspects" of the cases of the two men was ordered by the home secretary, Major Gwilym Lloyd George. Rev Basil Andrews, who disappeared for two days after Spot's trial, while owing money for hotel bills, was ordered to Scotland Yard, where the 88-year-old retired parson then made a statement that was considered of vital importance to police. Known to owe money to bookmakers, the parson – along with many men from the criminal underworld, some known to have been involved in gang feuds – had volunteered vital information: the code of silence with regard to talking to police had seemingly been broken. A list of names was sent out to all ports and airports throughout Britain, whereby Scotland Yard should be contacted if any of those on the list tried to leave the country. When Rev Andrews was threatened in an anonymous phone call at the end of September 1955, the police put a round-the-clock guard on him. His statement had run into thousands of words and it was believed that certain underworld characters were concerned about what the parson had told police. Meanwhile, several men were under observation, and ports and airports continued to be on alert.

Then, in October that year, Rita Comer, the wife of Jack Spot, was being held on remand in Holloway Prison, north London, while two men, one from Mayfair and the other from London's East End, were held on remand in Brixton Prison. It followed an extensive police inquiry and all three were charged with conspiring to defeat the course of justice at the Old Bailey trial of Spot. The two men and 27-year-old Rita Comer were refused bail. Then, on 2nd November, it transpired that the evidence given by Rev Andrews was all lies. He hadn't even seen the knife fight between Comer and Dimes. He told Bow Street Magistrates Court that he'd entered the witness box having been offered £50 by Jack Spot's wife. In the dock, accused of conspiring to defeat the course of justice at the trial of Spot, were Rita Comer, Rev Andrews, Peter MacDonough and Bernard Schack, better known as Sonny the Yank from Stepney. Rev Andrews, described as a "sponger" by the prosecution, gave evidence for almost three hours. All four applied for bail, but it was refused.

Then Rev Andrews declared that he had been threatened by gang members, and that if they saw him his throat would be cut. He was giving evidence at the Guildhall in London on 4th November, in a case where Christopher Glinski, 34, was accused of having committed perjury at the Old Bailey trial. The hearings continued throughout 1955. Then, in December, Bernard Schack – also accused in the conspiracy trial – told a court that he had been warned before his arrest to "get a ship out of the country". Schack, 53, said the man who had warned him was called Hubby Distleman, described as a well-known informer. Schack alleged that, on the fifth day of Spot's trial at the Old Bailey – the trial at which Schack was accused of trying to pervert the course of justice – he had been told he was "in trouble".

On 7th December 1955, Rita Comer went home to put her

children to bed for the first time in seven weeks. She had been fined £50 for her part in bribing Rev Andrews to give false evidence at the trial of her husband. By then, three men were charged with conspiring with her. Morris (Moisha) Goldstein was given two years, MacDonough 12 months and Schack also 12 months.

Following the conspiracy trial, police then opened an inquiry into the acquittal of Jack Spot. After "justice had been done" and Spot had been acquitted there had been a party at his luxury flat in Marylebone, which had been attended by Goldstein, Schack, Rita Comer and the man himself – and it was here that the first suspicion of a conspiracy had been raised. Rev Andrews was seen to arrive outside Spot's flat in a taxi and it had aroused police suspicions. Many of the witnesses had failed to give firm evidence to the police of the fight between Spot and Dimes, having been too afraid to speak in fear of retribution. It transpired that there had been a revolt against Spot, who had controlled the only real gang operating in Soho in the mid-1950s. Many of the bookmakers around at the time were purely interested in racing and not the gang warfare that Spot thought necessary. Spot had liked the thought of being a gang boss and thought of himself as such. He had started organizing the collection of money to help the defence of London criminals on remand and, through this, his popularity had grown in London's underworld.

He was recruited by Billy Hill, another self-styled London gangster boss, to look after a number of gambling houses. When Hill "retired" Spot had tried to take over, but made one mistake: he started to cash in on the bookmakers. He went to tracks collecting money from the smaller bookies for hiring out pitches. Albert Dimes led a revolt on behalf of the bookies against Spot, and more and more bookmakers refused to pay the so-called "boss". It was this that had led to Spot's attack on Italian Albert.

In May 1956, Spot was slashed with razors by a gang of men. The attack placed his life in danger, with surgeons at St Mary's Hospital in Paddington fighting to save him. His face had been severely cut and it was feared that, even if he lived, he would lose the sight of one eye. He had been attacked outside his flat in London and it was believed that men had trailed him on the way home late at night before attacking him. Wife Rita described how about 25 men had set on her husband as they came home late and that no one came to their aid. She told how she had screamed and screamed and eventually the mob had driven away in cars, leaving her husband fighting for his life on the pavement. She swore vengeance against the thugs who had done it. A few days after the attack, Spot was recovering in hospital, lucky to still have his right eye and lucky to be alive.

Robert Warren, 28, was arrested in connection with the attack on Spot, and was charged with wounding with intent to do grievous bodily harm. The arrest came after Rita Comer attended an identification parade. The hunt continued for the other men involved in the attack. A second man, Frankie Fraser, was then charged. But, at the Old Bailey, Spot denied that he was attacked by either Warren or Fraser, despite his wife's evidence that the two men accused of attacking him were in the dock. Mrs Comer also declared that Billy Hill was behind the attack on her husband, and that he had hit her on the shoulder with the Irish shillelagh that he used to bash her husband. Warren and Fraser were convicted and both sentenced to seven years. Hill avoided arrest and conviction when police could find no evidence linking him to the attack.

In June 1956, Spot was arrested and charged with causing grievous bodily harm to Tommy "Bugsy" Falco, an associate of Billy Hill. Falco had been razor-slashed as he left a Mayfair Club and received 47 stitches to his arm and side. The attack saw three people put under police guard, including Rita Comer, Falco and Johnny Rice (who, along with Falco, had given information against Spot). Jack Comer, meanwhile, maintained his innocence and alleged that he had been framed. The conspiracy theory was then put before the court on 29th June 1956. It was suggested that four days before the slashing of Falco, five men had sat in a car in Frith Street and discussed how to frame Spot. There was talk of how Billy Hill had paid £500 for this to be achieved. The five men were said to include Billy Hill, Victor Russo (better known as Scarface Jock), Albert Dimes, Johnny Rice and Frannie Daniels.

Then, in July 1956, a small pasty-faced man in a dark-blue, double-breasted suit, wearing horn-rimmed glasses, stood in the witness box at the Old Bailey and proclaimed: "I am boss of the underworld." William Charles Hill, better known as Billy, came as a surprise witness for the prosecution of Spot in the trial for the slashing of Falco. Hill had been called as a rebuttal witness after the conspiracy theory. The boss of London's criminal underworld admitted to having 13 convictions against him, after evidence given by Russo who claimed that Hill had offered to pay him £500 for slashing Falco and then framing Spot. Russo claimed that he had wanted nothing to do with the job. However, Hill had told Russo that he would put him "in trouble" and that he had everything ready for the attack. Russo had told Hill to carry out the attack himself and save himself the £500. Russo then went to the police when he heard that Spot had been arrested over the slashing. Russo claimed that he had refused to carry out the attack on Falco because he didn't think it was worth it.

In the witness box, Hill denied that he had planned the attack to frame Spot and that he'd never been to Frith Street on the day that Russo said he had met him. On 18th July 1956 Spot was cleared of attacking Falco. As Spot walked free, a crowd of 200 dispersed from outside the Old Bailey when they heard the verdict. Underworld figures who had featured in the case were nowhere to be seen. Even Falco had been absent from court.

By the time that Jack Spot was detained in September 1957 in Quebec, Canada, he had allegedly allowed his business interests to be scaled down and apparently had "retired". This did not, however, help his financial situation: he was pictured at a bankruptcy hearing in January the same year. The Canadian immigration authorities had to decide whether or not he was a "fit person" to be allowed into the country. The one-time, self-confessed Soho gang boss was planning on a few months' stay in order to visit an invalid brother. It was possible that he might be given a temporary permit in order to visit his brother but, if this failed, then the former gangland boss would be deported immediately. His entry to Canada was refused.

The following year, Spot was attacked by a group of hired "thugs" who were recruited by friends of men in jail. The thugs were believed to have set fire to a London club where Rita Comer worked. The Highball, at Lancaster Gate in west London, was burned out on 15th August 1958 and there was no doubt that it was arson. Meanwhile, Scotland Yard received information that the fire-raisers had been recruited specially for the raid by men who held a grudge against Spot – although he and his wife were nowhere near the club at the time of the fire.

In 1984, Jack Spot sat ringside at a charity boxing match taking place at Elephant and Castle. He was 75 years old, and had been the closest that Britain had come to having an American-styled gangster chief controlling London's underworld. He'd held power on every racecourse in Britain, but it had brought him around 300 stitches to injuries he'd suffered over the years at the hands of rival gangsters. It had been 30 years since he'd been to a boxing match, before his notorious stabbing by a rival gang, which left him for dead with 13 wounds in his back, neck and lungs.

There are those who claim that Spot's attack on Dimes led to his eventual demise. Many gangsters believed that Spot would never have gone to meet with Dimes without a weapon and that the support for the Italian was far greater on the streets of London than it was for the self-styled king of the underworld. The life story of Jack

Comer – who died in March 1996 – was told in the book *Man Of A Thousand Cuts* and a feature film based on his life is in the pipeline.

Gangs and Crime Families

Birmingham Boys

William "Billy" Kimber, a Birmingham bookmaker and head of the Birmingham Boys, was found in a street close to King's Cross in London with bullet wounds in his side on 28th March 1921. He was taken to the Royal Free Hospital for treatment. The incident was the precursor to some of the worst violence between rival gangs that the capital had ever seen.

The Birmingham Boys, also known as the Brummagem Boys, were a turf gang who operated between London's criminal underworld and the north of England between 1910 and the 1920s. For years they ruled with terror and intimidation, but they lost control of the southeast racecourses to the Sabini Brothers, headed by Charles "Darby" Sabini, who ended up dominating the London underworld and the racecourses across the southeast of England for much of the early part of the 20th century.

During Sabini's heyday he had extensive connections that included politicians, police and judges, and an alliance that rested on Jewish bookmakers and the Italians. However, in 1940, Sabini was arrested and held as an "enemy alien". He was released in

1942, but in 1943 was found guilty of receiving stolen goods and sentenced to three years in prison. By 1945, Sabini had lost his strong hold on his territory, which was first taken from him by Alf White and his gang, before gangsters such as Billy Hill and Jack Spot moved in and claimed the racecourses as their own.

Back in 1921, Billy Kimber concentrated on the only form of gambling left in England following the Gaming Act 1845: the horses. With excursion trains built specially for the races, all levels of society were known to enjoy the days out on offer, where bookies surrounded themselves by bodyguards in order to avoid protection rackets. However, Kimber and his gang controlled racecourses in the Midlands and the north of England, and set up another base in north London so that they could concentrate on racetracks across the southeast. He worked his way in with other gangsters, including those in the Hoxton Gang and the Elephant and Castle Gang, in order to take further control; bookies from the East End of London became a particular target. The then underworld boss Edward Emmanuel became involved and turned to Sabini's gang to provide protection. In March 1921, the Birmingham Boys ambushed the Italian gangster at Greenford Trotting Park, which led to Kimber's shooting. After this, violence between the two rival gangs escalated culminating in a car battle near Ewell in Surrey.

Kimber and his gang believed that Sabini's gang were travelling towards Epsom on Coronation Cup day – the event had been established in 1902 to commemorate the coronation of King Edward VII. They planned to ram the car from a side road, where they waited in a vehicle with its engine running. As the rival gang got nearer, Kimber's gang edged towards the road in order to collide with the opposing car side-on. However, the men in the car they hit were, in fact, a group of bookmakers from Leeds and a fight ensued between the two groups, who had weapons including axes and hatchets. Seven men were injured and taken to the nearby Epsom and Ewell Cottage Hospital while a large number of Kimber's gang were arrested. It was reported that more than 60 men had attacked the Leeds bookies as they were ambushed, most of whom escaped at the time on a coach that had been patiently waiting with its driver for the affray to be over. More than 23 of Kimber's men were arrested and, on 10th June 1921, a procession of cars containing prisoners left Brixton Prison for Epsom for hearing proceedings.

A total of 27 men were brought before Mr Justice Rowlatt on 19th July 1921 on charges of committing serious injury and being in possession of firearms. The prosecution alleged that the defendants had travelled from Birmingham in a charabanc on 30th May and that, three days later, they attacked a group of 10 bookmakers from Leeds with weapons including bricks, choppers, hammers and pistols.

That was not the end of the violence, though, as the following month saw similar weapons being used before a race meeting in Bath. Several bookmakers were attacked by men carrying hammers, choppers, sticks and large pieces of iron, and were treated for severe scalp wounds and abrasions at the Royal United Hospital. Charles Bird, a 20-year-old bookmaker's clerk from Long

Acre, stated: "It is all part of the old feud between London and Birmingham men which has been going on for years and years." He also described how he recognized several men from the affray in Epsom two months earlier.

The man in charge of the Epsom arrests was Detective Stevens, who virtually closed down the Birmingham Boys. However, it left the way wide open for the Sabini gang, who grasped their chance with both hands.

Hoxton Mob

Despite the demise of the Birmingham Boys in the 1920s, the Hoxton Mob – who had formed an alliance with the gang from the Midlands – continued with their racketeering. In June 1936, however, newspaper reports detailed "a very bad case", which occurred at Lewes racecourse in Sussex. The Hoxton Mob had travelled down from London and reached their intended destination just before 1.00pm. Almost immediately, two men had been extremely badly assaulted, one of whom was rushed to hospital. A total of 16 men from an estimated group of 30 were now in the dock facing charges at Lewes Crown Court. Displayed in the courtroom were a formidable collection of weapons including hatchets, truncheons, knuckledusters, hammers and chisels. All of the accused denied their guilt. However, on the day of the attack, Detective Sergeant Collyer had followed the 30-strong gang – including the 16 accused – to the back of the stand, where one of them – James Spinks from Hackney – shouted: "There they are boys." All the men began to run, with Collyer and a companion following suit.

Their targets were Alfred Solomon (an unfortunate bookmaker who had been targeted and injured during the Birmingham Boys' disturbance in Bath in August 1921) – who walked towards the gang carrying a bookmaker's stand – and the badly injured Mark Frater. In court, Collyer confirmed that as soon as the gang had got close enough to their targets Spinks had shouted and every member of the gang had produced a weapon. Spinks had flourished a hatchet over his head and Solomon received several blows from the men crowding around him. Collyer actually witnessed Spinks hitting Frater with the hatchet; more blows were dealt out by several other gang members. All 16 men were remanded. The men were then charged at Sussex Assizes, where the press described: "An extraordinary story – rivalling a gangster film scene – of an alleged attack by a crowd of men on two others." According to John Flowers, the prosecutor when the case began on 27th July 1936, the dangerous weapons used in the gangland fight were to be shown during the hearing. In the dock were George Gilder, 28, George Gardiner, 30, John Tyler, 27, George Churchill, 29, Thomas Mack, 40, James Spinks, 29, Arthur Boniface, 28, and Michael Illingworth, 28. Standing alongside them were Harry Bond, 25, Henry Wilkins, 23, Leslie Hain, 26, Joseph Kilby, 26, Stephen Bennis, 33, Timothy Bennis, 28, Albert Blitz, 24, and Charles Spring.

They were accused of wounding both Solomon and Frater, riotously assembling and assault. All pleaded not guilty. The court heard how Solomon ran from the scene after he was injured, but that Frater was not so lucky when a blow from Spinks' hatchet caused him to fall to the ground. Spinks was alleged to have shouted: "Let him have it." As the police descended on the scene, all the men ran.

At the end of July, a warning went out to all the gangsters living in England who lived by terrorism and intimidation on the racecourses, given by Justice Hillbery at Lewes Assizes when the 16 men were all convicted and given terms of imprisonment, ranging from 18 months' hard labour to five years in prison. The men had been found guilty on two charges of maliciously wounding, riotous assembly and assault. They stood herded together in the small dock, tight-lipped and motionless as the stern voice from the bench condemned gang violence.

The London gangsters had been sent down in cars from the East End to "beat up" the injured men. They were told by the judge: "You got together as a gang to assault and inflict bodily harm on this man Frater." The judge announced to the court that it had been a mercy that Frater had not been killed. The judge then commended the alertness of the police officers in the case and told the court how crimes of gang violence in Britain would be met with no mercy. The judge asked that all the convicted men should clearly understand that, and that the message should be conveyed to their friends, gang members and associates. Nearly all the men had several previous convictions for assault on the police, unlawful wounding and crimes of violence. The judge said he hoped that the sentences they received would show them, once and for all, that being a gangster and part of a gangland culture would bring them no mercy.

On 31st July 1936, the day after the men were convicted, threats to "get" Collyer from Brighton CID resulted in a special close watch for more trouble. The men who received sentences would be avenged by other members of the Hoxton Mob, it was believed. The full story hadn't been disclosed in court for legal reasons, but

Scotland Yard and Sussex police were co-operating to prevent gang warfare flaring up at Brighton racecourse in early August. Chief Inspector Sharpe, of Scotland Yard, was said to have known every racecourse gang crook by sight, and was due to attend Brighton races with a force of hand-picked men. Meanwhile, Sussex police were drafting officers from all over England to be there.

The man suspected of being behind the attacks at Lewes sat in an office in London's East End while the judge denounced the gangsters, including Jimmy Spinks, one of the attack's leaders. The man left behind in London was suspected of ordering the gang to "beat up" bookmaker Solomon and his clerk, Frater. When his gang were sent down, a man slipped from the court to give him news over the phone. He controlled a force of tic-tac men, racecourse touts and gangsters. When a bookmaker refused to pay for "protection", it was well known that he would end up in hospital.

A gangster who knew each of the sentenced men told a newspaper reporter that: "It [all] started two years ago in a pub in Tottenham Court Road." A young Jewish lad had slashed one of the East End boys with a razor blade. As a result, a fight ensued at Liverpool Street Station, where the Hoxton Mob met with a Jewish crowd and razors and iron bars were used by both sides. The men involved all escaped before the police arrived, and the gangsters then descended on Lewes racecourse looking for the young Jewish man who began the initial attack. However, Solomon and Frater became easy targets when the lad – who had gone away for "health reasons" – could not be found.

Ronnie and Reggie – the Kray Twins

In February 1965, Ronnie and Reggie Kray – probably Britain's most well-known and notorious gang leaders – found themselves in court facing charges of demanding money with menaces from a West End club owner for protection. Ronald Kray was also charged with possessing an offensive weapon, a sheath knife, and along with freelance writer Edward Smith, 32, was sent for trial at the Old Bailey. All three men pleaded not guilty.

The long-time rivals of Charlie Richardson had been arrested by Chief Superintendent Gerrard – one of Scotland Yard's "big five" – who told the brothers: "I have been making a number of inquiries and, as a result, I am going to arrest you for demanding money with menaces." Apprehended at Glenrae Hotel, Finsbury Park in north London, the brothers shouted to their older brother Charlie Kray to get them a brief. While in custody at Highbury Vale police station, a sheath knife was found in Ronnie's hip pocket. Asked what the knife was for, Kray replied: "I just have it, you know. It's nothing."

Eight days later, when Gerrard caught up with Smith, he denied he'd been with the Krays. Ivan Lawrence, defence for the Krays, and Kenneth Richardson, defending Smith, submitted that the prosecution had failed to establish a case for trial. However, the magistrate, Neil McElligott, disagreed and said he was satisfied that there was a case to go to trial. On 10th February, the brothers were refused bail by Lord Chief Justice Parker and two other judges in the high court. A similar application had been refused by Judge Griffith-Jones just a few days earlier and the Krays, described as company directors, awaited trial at the Old Bailey alongside Smith. The brothers had offered £18,000 in bail and would have willingly surrendered their passports. They had even offered to report to the police twice a day and undertook not to interfere with witnesses, but their QC, Peter Crowder, did mention that if they were granted bail then they would be in a position to trace witnesses. It took just two minutes for the judges to refuse bail.

In March 1965 Hew McCowan, the son of a baronet who accused the Kray brothers and Smith of demanding "protection" money, agreed in court that he had been a prosecution witness in three previous blackmail cases. McCowan, former part-owner of the Hideaway Club in Soho, London, also agreed that all the previous cases involved allegations of homosexual behaviour. He was asked by the defence counsel acting for 31-year-old Reggie Kray if he thought he was unmasking people who he thought had not behaved correctly. The reply came that he was not trying to unmask anyone, and he said that in two of the cases four men were convicted at the Old Bailey on charges of demanding money from him with menaces. In the third case, a man from Glasgow was freed by the Scottish verdict of "not proven".

The defence tried to make out that McCowan was a pathological liar who enjoyed the limelight and wanted to be part of a case involving the Krays. In April, the brothers, along with Smith, were found not guilty and discharged from the trial. The three had pleaded not guilty and, before the prosecutor could begin his closing speech, the judge intervened and said: "The case for the prosecution relied on the evidence of one witness, Mr McCowan." He then added: "If all of you think McCowan is not a reliable witness, you could not, with full confidence, be sure of the guilt of the accused. It is up to you under those circumstances to tell me you do not wish to hear any more, and return a verdict of not guilty." The jury then retired for seven minutes before the foreman announced that they did not wish for the case to continue. After leaving the Old Bailey, the Kray twins and Smith signed a statement at their solicitors' office in the City and it was said that they were taking legal advice on the question of high court writs being issued for false arrest and malicious prosecution. As the brothers' Jaguar pulled up outside their mother's house in Vallance Road, Bethnal Green, Reggie was greeted by 21-year-old Frances Shea, the woman in his life, while Charlie stated that: "Something is going on with our lawyer. All of us have been told not to say anything about the trial."

In August the following year, the brothers were back in the press after they spent long sessions early in the month helping with police inquiries into a murder at the Blind Beggar pub in Whitechapel Road. Ronnie and a friend had both taken part in an identity parade during his 36 hours at Commercial Street police station in Stepney. But he was released when two men failed to identify him. Reggie had spent 40 hours at Leyton police station, where a witness was missing so he was not required to stand in a line-up. The murder victim was 38-year-old George Cornell – one of Charlie Richardson's gang – who was shot dead while he enjoyed a drink in the Blind Beggar. He was known to both Krays, but they were adamant that the first they knew of his death was when they read about it in the newspapers. The Krays were called by Scotland Yard to see if they could help with inquiries. Reggie said: "It's getting a bit strong, the coppers involving us in all this."

It sounded as if the brothers had never put a foot wrong but, in April 1967, they were described as "notorious characters" at the Old Bailey, and "persons of the worst possible character" by Crown counsel John Mathew, who noted that they had convictions between them for "violence, blackmail and bribery". The activities of the brothers, Mathew continued, were always of interest to the police. Ronnie was to have been a prosecution witness at the trial of Detective Sergeant Leonard Townsend, 36, who was accused of attempting to obtain £50 from Ronnie as an inducement to show favour and of corruptly accepting £50 through a pub landlord for showing favour to Ronald Kray. Townsend pleaded not guilty to both charges and Mathew told the jury that, after making a complaint against the detective, Kray later refused to give evidence for the prosecution and then disappeared. He had not been found, though an arrest warrant was issued by an Old Bailey judge so that he could be brought to court as a witness. But, even if he did not appear, evidence could still have been put to the jury, as a tape-recording of the actual attempt to obtain money from Kray was taken at the Bakers' Arms in Hackney in August 1966. Kray had contacted a private detective and a tape recorder was hidden in a box of crisps. Kray was also fitted with a personal tape recorder, with a microphone hidden under his shirt. In the recording, it was alleged Townsend said he appreciated that Kray needed a little place to work quietly – in the pub – and that the police officer asked for some rent: a pony (£25) a week each for himself and another officer. Eventually, it was arranged that Townsend should collect £50 at a rendezvous with the pub licensee. This was arranged with co-operation from the police, who were closing in on Townsend.

But, in May 1968, it was Ronnie and Reggie who the police closed in on, when they were among 20 men detained by Scotland Yard. A total of 100 detectives and 20 police officers had taken part in a series of raids, which turned out at that time to be one of the biggest and most secret operations in the Yard's history. The first call was to the Kray twins and their brother Charlie at dawn. All three were detained at the home of their mother in a council flat on the ninth floor of Braithwaite House in Finsbury. They were taken to West End Central police station while the flat was put under police guard. The twins – who had notable records as amateur boxers – were part of the swoop by police following two years of intensive undercover activities by Scotland Yard detectives, directed by John du Rose.

The Krays were being held after being accused of plotting to murder "a male person", which prompted their lawyer, Paul Wrightson, QC, to find out who the alleged victim actually was. But, before he could find out, he was thwarted by David Hopkin, QC, who told the magistrate that he didn't see why – at that stage – the name should be given. Hopkin stated that he was not in possession of the name and that Wrightson should apply to the director of public prosecutions for the answer he sought. Wrightson demanded that the prosecution should give the name of the alleged victim before the case was sent for trial. The twins were facing two charges of conspiracy to murder, alongside Thomas Cowley, 32, while Charlie Kray was accused with his brothers of demanding money with menaces and other crimes.

Later in May 1968 the twins were accused – with Charlie – of helping to arrange the escape of Frank Mitchell, known as the "Mad Axeman", from Dartmoor Prison. They were also alleged to have harboured the escaped man 17 months previously, alongside four other men. They were still on remand on two charges of conspiring to murder the "male person" but, for a second time, the defence tried in vain to find out the name of the alleged murder-plot victims. The defence was given permission to press for the names by Lord Chief Justice Parker and two other judges on 18th June 1968. Ronnie and Reggie, along with Thomas Cowley, had charges that related to 1967 and 1968, while Richard Morgan, 35, was accused of the 1968 conspiracy. On six occasions, magistrates at Bow Street had refused to order the police to name the men, as Kenneth Jones, QC, for the director of public prosecutions argued that the names had been kept secret for "security" and because of possible witness tampering. The accused were given the names by the end of June via their counsel.

In July, the "fiendish" plot by the Krays for a man to be killed with a hidden poison syringe as he sat in the Old Bailey was then described to a court, while Kenneth Jones also produced a crossbow with a telescopic lens that he said was to have been used in another murder. While the name of one murder victim was kept secret, it was alleged that the Krays also planned to kill "Greek George" Caruana using guns, crossbow or gelignite. It was alleged that the Krays employed men called Cooper and Elvey to carry out the murders, but that neither of the intended victims had been murdered. Jones described a meeting between the Krays, Cowley and Cooper in a pub in Bethnal Green, where Reggie had explained that the man they needed to be killed would be difficult to get at.

The plan was to get the man in a place where he felt safe; and that was suggested as the Central Criminal Court itself, where he had been due to appear. The price for murdering the man was stated as £1,000 and it had been up to Cooper to decide how to successfully kill him. The idea muted by the men had been to use poison, which could be injected from a device on a briefcase. Cooper then contacted a man called Squire Waterman, who made the device. Counsel then produced a brown leather briefcase, which had clips inside designed to hold a hypodermic syringe that protruded from a hole in one edge of the case. The case had been designed to swing into contact with a person, then a ring under the handle was to be pulled, which would release the spring on a plunger that would inject the poison. The Krays were allegedly given a demonstration of the case in a London hotel and stated that it was just what they wanted. The poison was to be hydrogen cyanide. Cowley then showed Cooper who the target was, but Elvey was lined up to do the actual killing. However, whether his nerve failed him, or the briefcase weapon wouldn't work, the murder didn't take place and Cooper reported back to the Krays that Elvey had found it impossible to carry out the killing; there had also been too many people about.

The crossbow was intended for George Caruana and was chosen because it was accurate and silent. The second alleged murder conspiracy ended in April 1968 with Elvey being arrested at Glasgow Airport in possession of six sticks of gelignite. In his car, there was also a piece of paper with the registration of Caruana's car written on it. Kenneth Jones, QC, claimed that, 10 days before, Ronnie had called Cooper to a pub to discuss the murder and, on another occasion, Kray explained that Greek George was causing irritation to a club owner. Elvey was chosen as the man for the job and was given £100 to buy the weapon/weapons to do the deed. Cooper then co-operated with the police to set up a trap in a nursing home, where he invited the Krays to a meeting. They sent Cowley, who heard Cooper repeat details from all the conversations he'd had with the Krays. The twins were protecting club owner Bernie Silver from Greek George because, by doing him a favour, they would earn themselves a large equity in a club in London. They were also in some form of partnership for collecting money for Silver, and felt responsible for the actions of someone trying to muscle in on their partner. However, the case against the twins was dismissed on 23rd July 1968.

They were back in the limelight in September that year when it was alleged that, for 18 months, the three Kray brothers had lurked behind "front men" who ran five fraudulent companies for them. The brothers had drawn thousands of pounds from the firms, the prosecution claimed at Bow Street Magistrates Court, and had used violence, threats of violence and other means to get their own way. The brothers were among 13 men accused of conspiring to cheat and defraud. Others facing charges were Robert Buckley, David Levy, Thomas Welch, Samuel Lederman, Michael Fawcett, Harold Clarke, Frederick Bird, Alfred Willey, David Forland and John Chappell. The Krays were also accused of demanding a total of £5,500 with menaces from two of their alleged front men, Leslie Payne and Frederick Gore. Kenneth Jones, QC, once again prosecuting, listed the Kray companies for the court and stated that the brothers had obtained large amounts of cash, goods and services, to the value of many thousands of pounds: all obtained by fraud. Meanwhile, the twins were incensed that their grandparents had been questioned by the police and their pension books confiscated.

Jones then declared how he would illustrate how Ronnie and Reggie dealt with anyone who dared to gainsay them. Such people, he claimed, lived in fear of violence either to themselves or their families. When one of the managers of one of the Krays' "companies" (who had seen stock disappearing on a regular basis from the stores) decided not to go to work one Monday morning, the twins turned up at his house with Welch and punched the man in the stomach. When the man threatened the brothers with the police if they carried on in the same vein, he was pushed into their car and later pushed out of the vehicle on to the street. The brothers also used threats of violence to make Gore pay up £500 from the bank; and Payne was ordered to give them £5,000 when they discovered that he had £10,000 in a company that had nothing to do with them.

Then, on 15th October 1968, a court was told how one witness saw the killing of "Jack the Hat". The music was turned up in a flat where the murder was to take place in order to drown out the noise of a shot, stated Ronald Hart. When the gun held by Reggie did not go off, Ronnie held the victim and asked his brother to kill him. Reggie then stabbed Jack McVitie with a knife until he was dead. The twins and four other men were accused of murdering Jack the Hat; and four other men, including Charlie Kray, were charged with being accessories after the fact. The court was told that McVitie had not been seen at his home in Stratford, east London, since he left it on 28th October 1967 and that he was killed in cold-blood in the early hours of the following morning. Charlie Kray was alleged to have disposed of the body.

Hart told the court how McVitie had tried on several occasions to escape the Krays' grip before he died, but it had been impossible for the man to get away. Kray had pulled the trigger of the gun more than once, according to Hart, but it refused to fire. McVitie had then tried to jump from a window and had even broken the glass, but he was pulled back by Ronnie, Reggie and Hart. The victim was then mercilessly stabbed to death.

Hart had come forward in order to save his own skin, but had expected to be charged with murder alongside the twins and the other men. Those accused shouted from the dock that Hart was a well-known liar, but the woman whose basement flat McVitie had been killed in told the court that she had come home to find men cleaning her home. "Blonde Carol" Skinner also found bloodstains in the flat in Stoke Newington, north London. She testified that one of the accused, Ronald Bender, was coming from the basement with her little boy's socks over his hands. Another of the accused, Christopher Lambrianou, was also wearing socks over his hands and carrying her blue plastic washing-up bowl. Mrs Skinner was convinced that there was blood in the bowl and, despite the fact that the men scrubbed and cleaned her flat, she later found blood spots on the edge of the carpet. The Krays were then sent for trial with others at the Old Bailey on a charge of murdering Jack McVitie. All except one man, Anthony Barry, 30, were remanded in custody.

In early January 1969, John Dickson, a man alleged to have been a bodyguard for the Krays, pleaded guilty to harbouring Frank "Mad Axeman" Mitchell, who had escaped from prison. Dickson was sentenced during the first day of the hearing in which the twins, their brother and five other men faced charges arising from Mitchell's escape. Prosecuting counsel described a highly organized operation. Mitchell was allegedly shot dead in December 1966. Meanwhile, Ronnie Kray and John Barrie, 31, pleaded not guilty to murdering George Cornell at the Blind Beggar pub in 1966, and Reggie denied being an accessory. The third murder charge concerned Jack McVitie.

On 9th January, the jury heard how Reggie had killed McVitie in order to show off to his twin. Ronnie was alleged to have already carried out a murder, that of George Cornell. Reggie had decided to show his brother that he was his equal, and bookie's clerk McVitie was chosen as the target.

In the courtroom, Cornell's death was described first. It had been quiet in the saloon of the Blind Beggar and the victim sat at the corner of the bar, drinking with friends and chatting with a barmaid. Ronnie and Barrie walked into the pub and took out their guns, firing at Cornell. Terrified customers ducked out of sight, the barmaid fled to the cellars, and the two gunmen turned and walked out. Ronnie's bullet had gone into the victim's forehead. Barrie's two shots had hit no one. The barmaid, who was willing to give evidence, had seen Ronnie before and knew him by sight. She later identified Barrie. Other witnesses included three brothers who turned up at another pub to have a drink with Reggie. He explained to them what had happened. "Ron has just shot Cornell", he said.

The court then heard how McVitie had gone out for a drink on the night he was killed and was found by the Krays in Stoke Newington. Anthony Barry, the manager of the club in which they all met up, refused to let the Krays murder the man on the premises so they went to the flat in Evering Road instead. Barry gave the brothers a gun and then left. The gun wouldn't fire but McVitie realized that he was doomed. Terrified, he broke the flat window in a desperate bid to escape but was pulled back. Ronnie held the victim from behind while Reggie stabbed him to death with a carving knife. As Ronnie shouted "Kill him Reg", McVitie fell to the floor dying, but Reggie then plunged the knife into the victim's neck twice, twisting it each time. Meanwhile, jailed John Dickson said in mid-January 1969 that he had decided to give evidence against the twins because the murders had to stop.

Dickson claimed to have driven Ronnie to the Blind Beggar pub when Cornell was killed and was adamant that, together with Barrie, the twin had carried out the murder. He even admitted that he'd given Ronnie a false alibi. He also stated that Jack the Hat was harmless and then said: "Somebody has got to have the guts to come forward and say their piece, and let ordinary people know what cruel bastards they really are." He also relayed how McVitie had been a personal friend of the Krays and that what they had done to him was cold-blooded and senseless.

The Krays, it was claimed, had even threatened to have Blonde Carol and another woman named Vicky (Hart's girlfriend) poisoned if they talked about the murder of McVitie. Ronnie Kray had a woman on standby to kill the two women if need be and she had also been asked to "get rid" of Cornell's wife too if necessary. Hart also admitted in court that he had once shot a man named John Sheay on the orders of Ronnie Kray because he had shown up Dickson in a fight. He had been ordered to kill, but he just shot him in the hand. He said: "When Ronald Kray tells you to do something, you do it – because if you don't you get shot yourself." Asked why he had helped to hold McVitie so he could be killed, Hart replied: "I know the Kray twins ... if I had not tried to help them, I would have gone with him as well."

The twins were also well-known for their racketeering, which had been their main activity. The Krays and many other members of their gang lived on protection money known as a "pension". If people refused to pay, they were either hurt or people were sent to start fights. John Barry, brother of Anthony, had agreed to pay protection money of £50 a week. A pension was what the gang called regular protection money; "nipping" was when they helped themselves to whatever it was that they wanted. The Regency Club – where McVitie had been drinking prior to being lured to his death – was subjected to nipping on a regular basis until a regular pension had been established. Gang members didn't pay for their drinks when they had parties at the club.

Ronnie Kray claimed at the hearing in February 1969 that the police were ordered by the Home Office to arrest him on any pretext and to make sure he was found guilty of the two murders. On day 18 of the hearing, Blonde Carol was accused by the men on trial of watching too many Dracula films when she told the court how she'd found blood in her flat and had seen Lambrianou carrying a bowl of blood from her home. The same day, Anthony Barry confirmed how he had paid the Krays for protection but never received anything in return. He said: "We had to pay it in case we got trouble in the club. But the only trouble we ever had was from them." Barry, a partner in the Regency Club, denied having any involvement in the death of McVitie, apart from taking the gun to the flat because he was too frightened to do otherwise. Barry had known the Krays for eight years and knew that when they entered his club, most people would drink up and leave. Over the years, the twins and their gang – known as the Firm – had got through thousands of pounds worth of drink, but they never paid for a drop and Barry knew better than to ask for the money. But, on 20th February, Reggie's counsel, Paul Wrightson, asked the jury to consider how unfortunate it was to be a Kray twin. In his closing speech, he told the jury that it was a case of Reggie being guilty by association and he particularly objected to the expression "the Kray twins". Lambrianou's defence team argued that he was not a member of the "Firm".

After 39 days of trial, Ronnie and Reggie were convicted of murder and the Kray firm was finally out of business. The 35-year-old twins and eight henchmen then faced sentencing at the Old Bailey. Ronnie was convicted of two killings, while Reggie was only convicted of the McVitie murder, although he was found guilty of being an accessory in the Cornell killing. Charlie Kray was convicted of being an accessory in the McVitie murder. The only man who was acquitted was Anthony Barry.

The "Firm" had operated based on fear. As long as people were frightened enough, then the Firm was in business. To the Firm, killing was part of normal business dealings; it was a prestige booster. Intimidation was their trade. It brought them cash from other people's legitimate businesses; it was the Firm's protection against reprisals. In order to stay on top in the terror trade, the

Krays had to be the most terrifying of all.

George Cornell had been a vulnerable member of the Richardson gang once his own gang had all been sent down after the "torture" trial in 1966. He had been found drinking on Kray turf and it was only a matter of time before he was subjected to their terror. For 21 months after the Cornell killing, fear worked overtime for the Firm. At the inquest, no one came forward to identify the gunmen. Yet, everyone knew who had shot the Richardson gang member. Then, as the case began to fade from the headlines, Ronnie was agitated for another spot of cold-blooded murder and he was overheard to say to his brother: "I've done my one. It's about time you did yours."

When McVitie was killed, the Firm thought they were untouchable. They ordered their minions to clean up the mess, clothes were destroyed, the murder knife was thrown in a canal along with the faulty pistol. But, the fortunes of fear were beginning to run out. The barmaid from the Blind Beggar showed enormous courage as she took on the Krays and gave evidence against Ronnie, whom she recognized as the killer. Hart, too, began to talk as did former bodyguard Dickson. Slowly but surely the stronghold the Firm thought they had was beginning to unravel. As courage gained a foothold, others began to come forward from the underworld and its fringes for the first time, willing to tell what they knew. The Firm, which had prospered on fear, was forced into liquidation by the courage of others.

It had all seemed so different when, on 24th October 1933, a little after 8.00pm, Violet and Charles Kray, already the proud parents of Charlie Kray, celebrated the birth of their twin boys, whom they named Ronald and Reginald. These cherished sons were to create an empire formed on fear, corruption, extortion, protection, torture and, finally, murder. The twins were identical except that Ronald, the younger of the two, had a mole on his neck.

They lived in a labyrinth of dark and dismal streets of tenements blackened with the grime of a century. It was the territory of London's top underworld crooks and home to poor families trying desperately to make an honest living. Poverty kept the tallyman busy, his customers constantly in debt, and it kept the queues outside the pawnbrokers' shops. Some family's bed sheets went into the pawnbrokers on Monday in order to buy the week's groceries and were redeemed on Friday. Despite the general poverty and unemployment, however, the street bookmakers flourished. Children roamed the streets at night, alert for mischief or stealing. They stayed until the pubs turned out, watched the inevitable boot or bottle fights, and then went home. In some places, the police patrolled in pairs. Local toughs carried choppers, clubs or bicycle chains. It was the breeding ground for tearaways and criminals and it affected everyone in the neighbourhood.

Where others struggled to break out of this corrupting environment, Ronald and Reginald Kray fitted into it perfectly and manipulated it. As boys, they joined the street gangs, fighting as all east London kids fought but with a built-in instinct for survival. The one thing that might have changed them was schooling, which they missed out on in part. They went to Daniel Street School in Bethnal

Green after their parents moved from Hoxton. But then came the Second World War and, with hundreds of other children, they were evacuated to Suffolk. The boys were sent to live with a doctor's family in a red-brick mansion in Hadleigh. Clare Styles was the wife of the doctor who looked after them. When they arrived, the twins were unable to read and Clare Styles spent long periods teaching them. Ronnie and Reggie returned to London while the bombing was still rife.

At that time, school was optional and they opted out; they preferred to roam the streets with gangs of children. It was then that the boys discovered that being identical could work in their favour. They provided alibis for each other when they got into trouble, and in fights they developed a plan that one held the victim while the other one bashed him. They went to work in Billingsgate fish market and for two years carried boxes of fish around. When they tired of that, they joined their father travelling around the Home Counties buying clothing. The evenings were spent standing around the street corners of Mile End with their gang. When people tried to walk along the pavements they were pushed into the road. If they complained they were punched. This was violence for fun, and they sometimes extorted five or 10 shillings from a frightened victim. But it wasn't enough.

The twins had too much steam to let off and too much latent violence that had to find an outlet. They found a legitimate way of doing this and became boxers. Charlie Kray was already shaping up well in the ring. The twins joined Mansford Amateur Boxing Club and later the Repton ABC. They were both skilled, quick and had devastating punches. At 16, they were involved in a street fight and Ronnie was taken to Bethnal Green police station for assaulting a policeman who had tried to move them off the pavement. Reggie rounded up a gang and they tried to fight their way in to rescue Ronnie. They were beaten back with black eyes and bloody noses and Ronnie was convicted. In 1951 they turned professional boxers and made their debut on their home ground of Mile End. Both won easily and, later, all three Krays appeared at the Albert Hall. But intimidation and bullying became a much easier way of making money.

At 18, Ronnie and Reggie were called up for national service. They reported to the Royal Fusiliers at the Tower of London but, that same day, attacked the sergeant in charge with their fists and went on the run. They assaulted a police officer and escaped arrest but were circulated as "wanted". Six months later they were picked up and sentenced to one month's imprisonment. They were then taken by the Army into custody for desertion. They overpowered their guards at Canterbury Barracks and escaped with two others. All four were later arrested and sentenced to nine months' detention. Demobilization saw them back in their old haunts with a formidable reputation.

Jack Spot was "King of the Underworld" at this time and the twins went to work for him at race meetings. Their average pay was £5 a day, but they had bigger plans in mind. They rented an old hut off Mile End Road and installed four billiard tables. Their tough reputation was growing fast, as was their collection of weapons. Next they set up a gambling house complete with cafe and a voluntary system of giving £5 to anyone discharged from prison. They then obtained a large terraced house on Mile End Road, which they converted into a luxurious club. Henry Cooper opened a gym on the first floor and it was here that the "Firm" would gather. The club was somewhere to avoid trouble with the police but it eventually closed after a series of police raids. But, by now, the twins had a dozen bodyguards and they partied around the East End like Al Capone. The reign of fear had begun in the square miles that they called "the Manor", their territory in the East End of London.

The arrest of the Firm and the tight security net thrown around prisoners, witnesses and jurors throughout the long trial was a masterpiece of police planning, carried out by a dedicated team. The operation started in September 1967, when Commander John du Rose sent for Detective Superintendent Leonard "Nipper" Read to join his team at Scotland Yard. His orders in his new role were simple: to investigate the activities of the Krays and other members of their gang. Nipper's team was handpicked and, on 7th May 1968, the police officers held an important meeting before swooping on the Firm. The team that protected the witnesses consisted of 78 officers, who virtually became family to some, while the jury members were protected by 58 detectives.

Reggie was sentenced to life for murder and taken to Brixton Prison. It was recommended that, like his brother, he should serve 30 years. Six of the Firm were given life sentences by the judge at the Old Bailey. Justice Melford Stevenson sent 10 men to jail for a total of 159 years. But the choice of which prison to send them to was a problem for the Home Office. Many of the Richardson gang were already housed in top-security prisons, while other prisons housed inmates connected with both gangs.

Meanwhile, in April 1969, Ronnie and Charlie Kray were acquitted of murdering Frank Mitchell, but Reggie and Freddie Foreman were still facing a murder charge. In May 1969 all three Kray brothers faced fraud and conspiracy charges.

Just less than a year later, crossed telephone wires brought to light an alleged kidnap plot in which the Krays had paid £50,000 to someone to take Princess Margaret's eight-year-old son, Viscount Linley. The boy would be given back in return for getting them freed from jail. If successful, Lord Linley would be freed after Ronnie and Reggie reached an island north of Australia. The businessman who heard the phone conversation went straight to Scotland Yard and the details of the plot were hatched at Parkhurst Prison. News of the planned kidnap was sent to the Queen in April 1970 as she visited Australia's capital, Canberra. It was said that the Queen kept in close contact with her sister, Princess Margaret, in London. Despite the crossed telephone wires, prison guards at Parkhurst had also heard about potential kidnapping plots and all prison schemes were dropped. However, there was never any evidence to suggest that the Krays had been in on planning a kidnapping.

In October 1972, Leslie Payne – the man who had first grassed on the Krays – went to prison for five years for attempting to obstruct the course of justice in two trials involving stolen cars. He had decided to shop the Krays after he heard they had put a price of £5,000 on his head.

Ten years later, Ronnie and Reggie were allowed briefly out of prison to attend their mother's funeral. A petition calling for the release of the twins had been handed to the Home Office a year before in 1981, but officials at Parkhurst Prison where Reggie was held still considered him likely to be dangerous if he was released, while doctors at Broadmoor did not consider Ronnie fit to be released. In 1983, the twins mourned the death of their father, Charles. Neither attended his funeral because they did not want a repeat of the media circus that had blighted their mother's farewell, but they were secretly reunited in 1984 for their 51st birthday. The once brutal bosses in London's underworld exchanged gifts and cards and ate a celebration lunch at Broadmoor Prison for the criminally insane.

On 17th March 1995, Ronnie Kray died of a heart attack at the age of 61. A crook who was tortured by him said: "I'm glad he's dead. He was the cruellest man that ever walked." Lennie Hamilton had been blinded with a red-hot poker as Kray laughed in delight. Chain-smoker Ronnie collapsed and died at Broadmoor top-security hospital, 27 years into his 30-year sentence, from which he had no hope of release. Small-time hoodlum Hamilton said: "When I heard Ronnie was dead it was as if a great cloud lifted. He was completely evil and if there's a God, he'll be on his way to hell now."

Hamilton still trembled when he remembered what had been

done to him at the Regency Club. He had been called to see Ronnie at the twins' club in Knightsbridge and shown through to the kitchen where a roaring fire in the grate was already heating up two sharpening steels and a poker. At first, they started burning the clothes off Hamilton, but then Ronnie pressed a red-hot steel into his cheek and rolled it along his cheekbone. Hamilton's hair was burnt off and his suit was set on fire. He thought he was going to die. Hamilton had his eyes closed, but Ronnie told him to open them. The red-hot poker was so close to Hamilton's eye that the blinding heat went straight through the eye and damaged the retina for good, permanently blindling him in one eye. He was repeatedly burned until he passed out. When he came round, he was burned again, despite the fact that he begged for mercy. Hamilton wasn't tortured for information, he was burned and blinded for fun, and to enable Ronnie to show others just how ruthless he was.

While some were glad that Ronnie's last breath was over, there were others who saw him as a modern Robin Hood. No one denied that he was a villain and a killer, but it was generally accepted that he only hurt his own. The Krays had never hurt old ladies or kids, according to former Richardson gang member Frankie Fraser. He said: "They were only violent to people like me." But, the Scotland Yard man responsible for bringing the twins to justice said: "They have been turned into a legend that they do not deserve. The truth is they were horrible, violent men who did terrible things to fellow humans."

At Ronnie's funeral in March 1995, Reggie sat handcuffed to a prison warder at St Matthew's Church in Bethnal Green. The church was packed to bursting with mourners and undercover police waiting for Ronnie's last grand entrance. One of the wreaths was an arch of flowers around a photograph of the Manhattan skyline and signed simply "New York". If it was a tribute from the Mafia, no one was saying.

Then in 1997, Charlie Kray, the wrong side of 70 and charged with masterminding a £78 million drugs ring, had unsuccessfully tried to convince the jury at his five-week trial that he was a harmless old man who had just been a small-time crook. He was found guilty.

Kray had forged links with several of America's most feared Mafia families. He had even written a book about how he and his brothers had played a major part in setting up links with some of America's most powerful underworld chiefs. The Krays had met with Angelo Bruno, head of the Philadelphia Mafia, at the Hilton Hotel in Park Lane, London and the two organizations struck a 50/50 deal to launder stolen bearer bonds worth $2 million. Charlie Kray then became friendly with Frank Sinatra's Mafia-linked bodyguard Eddie Pucci. They became so close that when Sinatra's son Frank junior was released after being kidnapped, Pucci brought him to London to be looked after by Charlie. The Krays opened another line of contact with the Mafia after meeting Tony "Ducks" Corello of the New York Lucchese clan. Charlie then travelled to New York to meet members of the Colombo crime family.

Charlie Kray died at the age of 73 on 4th April 2000. He lost his fight against heart disease just hours after Reggie had been allowed to visit him for a final goodbye. Just a few months later, Reggie was diagnosed with cancer and underwent emergency surgery before being released from prison on compassionate grounds by Home Secretary Jack Straw in August 2000 after 32 years behind bars. Having been officially released from jail on 22nd September 2000, Reggie Kray – the last surviving member of a criminal brotherhood that will undoubtedly never be forgotten – died on 1st October at the age of 66.

Each of the twins had had their favourite brand of violence. Reggie's was "the cigarette punch" – rivals were offered a smoke and Reggie would lean forward as if to light the cigarette, but then deliver a powerful uppercut breaking the victim's jaw. Ronnie preferred a flick knife or razor. But, in the end, it was a heart attack and cancer that finally closed the file on the grim legend that had been the Krays.

Mafia

The Mafia has been in existence for hundreds of years and is made up of many different "branches" and gangs the world over. As a secret society with a strong code and total commitment, it is beyond the scope of this book to do more than provide information that is already widely available in records and documented reports of individual cases and incidents. Some of the more well-known names and activities are also discussed.

One of the first newspaper reports to mention the Mafia in the 20th century came in March 1909 when Joseph Petrosino was shot in a street in Palermo, Sicily. The famous American detective had been on a secret mission to investigate the connection of the "Black Hand" secret society in New York but met his death when he was gunned down by assassins as he waited for a tram. The chief of the new Secret Service Corps, formed in February 1909, was dead and thus the society's most formidable opponent was no longer a threat. Petrosino, known as the "terror of the Black Hand", was shot four times near the Piazza Marina and his body found dead in the street. He had managed to fire one round at his assailants before his murder, which took place just a week after he arrived in Palermo. Two men were seen hurrying away from the scene by witnesses.

In New York, the assassination of Petrosino stirred the United States police force as nothing else had managed to do for a number of years. Orders were issued in all principal cities that any suspected members of the Black Hand gang should be arrested and questioned on a conspiracy that may have existed against the detective – and a relentless warfare was promised against the organization of blackmailers.

In Palermo itself, several arrests were made of former convicts who had previously been in the United States and two individuals in particular had come to the notice of local police. One was an international thief and the other a man with a "bad" reputation who had been involved in a series of crimes in New York. Both men had eventually left America following attempts by Petrosino to arrest them.

The Black Hand was an organization that had been terrorizing New York since 1901 and it was known to be directly associated with the Mafia. It was reported that the Black Hand was merely the Mafia duplicated in New York but, in America, where there were 50 men of wealth for every one in southern Italy, the organization had begun to flourish and prosper on a far greater scale with more widespread and criminal activities. Blackmail was a favourite practice of the Mafia, which the Black Hand had managed to carry to a pitch unparalleled in history.

Petrosino, otherwise known as Bull-Dog Joe, had been given a small force of men when the Black Hand first became notorious who were commissioned to break up all the Italian gangs it could find. Each time Petrosino arrested a gang member, he knew that it increased his own chances of being murdered and he never went out unarmed. Known for his cooking – which seemed to be the pastime he had outside work – he was quite convinced that he would die fighting and not of old age in his bed. Petrosino had received numerous death threats from those he was trying to shut down. Roosevelt, who knew Petrosino well, said: "Lieutenant Petrosino was a great and good man. I knew him for years. He did not know the name of fear."

The Black Hand or "Mano Nera" was a name derived from one of the grim signs used by the members of the organization on letters of warning, or to mark the bodies of their victims that an act of vengeance had been achieved. It was believed at the time of Petrosino's murder that the Black Hand, by means of murder threats, had managed to raise £20,000 each year since their infancy, although in the years up to 1909 things had not run quite as smoothly for them. They had bungled an attempt on an Italian bank in New York and their ringleader was shot dead by expert marksmen when their blackmailing efforts failed and they raided the financial centre.

At first, the Black Hand only blackmailed New York Italians, but it gradually extended its operations to other nationalities. Many people in New York suffered great stress and worry over the threatening letters they received from the organization, including revolver manufacturer and millionaire David Wesson, whose death was partly ascribed to the menacing letters he received and the stress and strain that this caused him.

However, despite the rise of the Mafia and the organizations associated with it, many still believed that gangster life in America was "invented" by imaginative Hollywood writers. That is, until Senator Kefauver, who in 1952 had a 30 per cent chance of succeeding Truman in the next presidential election, exposed the story of a crime-busting campaign that began when he became chairman of the Senate Crime Investigating Committee. Many thought that Senator Kefauver's book *Crime In America* was one of the best gangster thrillers in the mid-20th century and that, unlike the scripts from Hollywood, it was completely true. He put the spotlight on a nationwide crime syndicate, whose chiefs were impeccably dressed, white-collared businessmen, wearing "executive-type" rimless spectacles, and whose children went to the best colleges. These men had bought shares in famous American companies whose advertised brands were household names, and they controlled innumerable businesses from advertising to washing machines. They bribed and employed thousands of policemen and politicians.

The story for individuals involved in the crime syndicate usually followed a gangster who found himself with more money than he knew what to do with, accrued from illegal ventures in gambling, narcotics, bootlegging and prostitution. What next? Albert Anastasia of Murder, Inc. had gone into dress-manufacturing in New York. Longie Zwillman, the rum runner, had a tobacco-selling slot-machine company, a motor company and a company dealing in scrap iron. He also had investments in property and businesses under dozens of other names. Frankie Costello, an elder statesman of crime in New York, eventually ran a "legitimate" business, but he admitted to Kefauver that he had once received £7,000 a year from a British company to promote the sale of Scotch. He said that he used to "suggest" to certain bars that it would be good for them to sell particular whiskies. According to Kefauver, Costello's business was a convenient front. A New York syndicate member would think nothing of arranging for a colleague in Chicago or elsewhere to do him a favour and kill off a business competitor or collect a debt. Almost all of the syndicate "big shots" were Sicilians belonging to the Mafia, who enforced a code of death to anyone who resisted or betrayed it. Kefauver's committee went to New York to question Philip Mangano, brother of the "head" of the Mafia's New York organization. One month later, Mangano was found dead in a Brooklyn swamp. And, in Chicago, police chief Drury was brutally murdered before he could talk to the committee. Joe Fusco, vice president of a Chicago liquor firm, narrowly escaped death when he left the committee hearings. He had stated that he was personally worth $1 million and that his company was worth another couple of million. He said that he gave every cop in town a bottle or two of whisky at Christmas. After he left the hearings he missed being killed by a bomb: apparently, the Mafia didn't like the way he talked. C J Rich, who ran a betting agency, revealed how he got a famous telegraph company to act as his agents in 150 centres, but the committee discovered that gangster William Molasky was a principal shareholder in the telegraph company. And, a parson revealed that when he complained of all the gambling clubs in his neighbourhood he was immediately approached by one of the gangster-businessmen and offered funds for a new Sunday school building if he dropped his campaign. Alvin Glessey, a well-known Cleveland accountant, managed to limit the gangster's jail term to four years. When the gangster came out of prison he immediately hired Glessey as his tax adviser. James Adduci, a Chicago politician, was told by the Mafia that they would spend £38,000 defeating him when he next ran for election unless he voted against a particular crime bill. He did as he was told. The crime syndicate was everywhere and chiefs earned millions of dollars a year tax free.

United States authorities linked the evidence together and decided that the head of the syndicate was Charles "Lucky" Luciano, a notorious gangster who was expelled from America and settled in Sicily after being sent home as an undesirable. From a distance of 5,000 miles, Luciano was alleged to be running a crime empire unequalled in modern history. He was named as the "boss" of the Mafia, which had managed to seize and control a huge segment of US business.

In April 1969, leaders of the Mafia sat down together like a board of directors in order to study President Nixon's declaration of a new war on crime. Somewhere in the United States, the men who pulled in $5 billion a year from organized crime, gambling, prostitution, narcotics and loan-sharking, made more money than any giant corporation in America. For 30 years, their stock-in-trade had been terror and their members enforced "omerta" (the code of silence) by ruthless methods. Only outsiders called it the Mafia. To its members, it was La Cosa Nostra, meaning "our thing". And, in the late 1960s, this "thing" was raking in more money each year than it was costing to run the Vietnam War.

There were at least 5,000 hard-core members of the Mafia in the US and they were split into 24 families, who dominated the country from New York, where pickings were richest, to Los Angeles and San Francisco. The ruler of the family – the capo or boss – was backed by a number of caporegime or lieutenants. Each was in charge of a crew composed of "soldiers" whose actual status depended entirely on their experience, killing ability and general use to the organization. From the boss to the lowest soldier, one common factor united these men: they had to be Italian or of Italian descent. Outsiders were allowed to work for them and sometimes with them, but they could not ever become members of the Mafia, and the umbrella of legal and strong-arm protection was not extended to these people.

The Black Hand had threatened death or mutilation to the children of those who received their letters should they decide not to pay. Gangs fought each other, but rivalry did not reach its peak until the early 1930s when the underworld fought with machine guns in the streets of half a dozen American cities. Out of this carnage rose a bloody phoenix that was to become the modern Mafia of the late 1960s, open to Sicilians and Neapolitans alike and others of Italian descent. The inner workings of the Mafia in the United States were first given an airing at a televised hearing of the Senate Permanent Sub-Committee on Government Operation in 1963 when Joseph

Valachi, a Mafia turncoat who had been under sentence of death from the boss of his "family", described the structure and personnel of the secret brotherhood. More special agents were moved into the Mafia field and their efforts began to pay off. But still only a trickle of small-time Mafia soldiers went to jail.

The leaders were protected by crooked policemen, bent politicians and lawyers who seemed to always be one jump ahead of the prosecution. Unwittingly, even in 1969, every man, woman and child in America contributed to the Mafia coffers – from the milk they drank to the dimes the kids slipped into chewing-gum vending machines; the rake-off was relentless. The Mafia had infiltrated the labour unions and all types of businesses in a massive way; most of the small legitimate businesses were taken over by the Mob because their owners had fallen into debt. If a man's credit at the bank ran out, and he was desperate to save his business, he may have gone to or been approached by Mafia loan sharks. They were easy to find and, provided that the individual was desperate enough to pay an interest rate of 20 per cent, they were "helped". One week could mean paying 100 per cent interest on the initial loan, or the Mafia simply moved in and took what they wanted.

The organization was known to be involved in banking, milk, ice cream, trucking, air freight, hotels, refuse collection, jukeboxes, meat packing and distribution. It was even involved in window-cleaning. Many of these businesses had not been taken over by extortion, but simply by the Mafia investing its cash reserves on the stock market. In this way, it was able to take control of legitimate businesses. The men behind the machine were those who could afford the sharpest legal minds in the country; they also surrounded themselves with cunning accountants and top electronic experts who knew the ways of computers and government "bugging" devices. Faced with such criminal talent and the money at its command, President Nixon's new crime fighters were expected to have as little success as the American forces had against the Vietnamese.

The Mafia also wielded power in the showbiz industry. Not least, the respected Sinatra family were under investigation for having links to the organization. When Frank Sinatra's father died in January 1969, children were sent home from school, shops closed, banks locked their doors and the whole town of Fort Lee, New Jersey, went into mourning. Surrounded by broad-shouldered men with black hats and lacquered fingernails, the entire Sinatra clan attended the funeral service at the red-bricked Church of the Madonna. On the road outside, a high-ranking New York police officer deftly directed traffic for the funeral procession as a cortege of 37 limousines, complete with 150 lavish bouquets, drove slowly past. An honour guard of white-gloved firemen and 100 policemen stood by as Sinatra escorted his ageing mother, Natalie, from the church.

But, Fort Lee, in the State of New Jersey, presented the singer with an embarrassing problem. He would not be able to go home again. A warrant had been issued in New Jersey for his arrest, granted at the request of the State Commission of Investigation, which was investigating Mafia activities. New Jersey had long had a reputation of having a heavy concentration of Mafia bosses. In June 1969,

Sinatra had accepted a summons to testify before the Commission. He was ordered to appear on 14th August, but his Los Angeles lawyer, Milton Rudin, was granted a one-month postponement on his behalf due to certain business commitments. Neither Sinatra nor his lawyer ever called the Commission back and a warrant was duly issued. Unfortunately for Sinatra, he had perhaps been unable to choose his friends and associates on the way up in show business – and the Commission, it was speculated, wanted to question him about some men he was said to have rubbed shoulders with during his career. Six years previously, Nevada's Gaming Control Board had forced Sinatra to sell his interests in two gambling casinos because of his having entertained Salvatore "Sam the Plumber" Giancana, boss of the Chicago Mafia. Giancana, who later fled back to his native Italy, had been identified by American authorities as one of the nine members of the Mafia's national commission, the ruling body of organized crime. Sinatra and Dean Martin had both been mentioned in a tape-recording released by the FBI to *Life* magazine. These transcripts of bugged conversations involved Giancana and others who were heard discussing the difficulty of booking Sinatra and Martin into a nightclub the boss favoured. But in New Jersey, where the Sinatra family was extremely well respected, no one seriously thought that if Frank drove over from New York to visit his mother for a bowl of spaghetti that he would be arrested.

America's front-line fight against the Mafia continued. In October 1969, a man named Tony Renato, who was slim, dark and Italian born, hadn't been home to see his wife and children for a month. He hadn't even spoken to them, for Renato – not his real name – was an undercover detective who, along with 145 other experts, had been sent on one of the toughest assignments ever: to "smash" the Mafia. Renato, an FBI agent, worked alone like a wartime spy. There were no set hours, no time off and he slept in a downtown Chicago boarding house where the rest of the lodgers thought he was an ordinary working man. President Nixon had stated that he would go all out to end the Mafia's hold on American life and business. To do this he had asked Congress to provide more than double the annual anti-crime budget of £10 million. Renato and his 144 colleagues had their own name for these new moves against the Mafia. It was called Operation Tightrope: a delicate balance between making no mistakes and living – or being discovered and dying.

The men they were hunting were no strangers to murder. They were capable of thinking up new and improved refinements in killing with the same care as a chef creating a new dish. In Chicago alone, the police department estimated that there were at least 300 top-class criminals who worked full-time for the Mafia. They directed and controlled a far greater number of people involved in gambling, drug distribution, loan sharking, labour racketeering and acts of terrorism. Chicago had one of the biggest American Mafia families that the police were seeking to destroy. A chilling set of figures were released to the public: between 1919 and 1963 there were 976 gangland killings in the Chicago area, an average of 23 a year. In only two of these murders were the killers arrested and convicted. The 976 deaths were executions of competitors, those who were unable to pay their debts and men who turned informer. And Renato's role? To find informers, because infiltrating a family would be virtually impossible.

The Mafia men were all well known to each other. Their security was tight. Thus Renato knew that the men he wanted were on the fringe. He'd studied their photographs, memorized their habits and wanted to infiltrate those around the edges who ran errands for the big bosses. They carried drugs and stolen property, delivered messages and threats. Some of them collected money or beat up those who paid late. They were the Mafia men who did the dirty work, but sometimes the fear of vengeance became even too great for them and they turned informant.

Renato never went near any police stations. In order to feed back information he called his chief on a special number from public telephone boxes. He was also given instructions in this way. As a result of Renato's work and that of his colleagues, more than 60 arrests had been made by the end of the decade. However, it was an extremely small dent in the armour of a huge, well-oiled machine. Of the 24 Mafia families targeted by police, five were located in New York, such were the rich pickings in the city. For Renato and his colleagues on the tightrope, it was a lonely job. However, for the first time, the authorities had managed to gain a substantial amount of money in order to deal with the problems and were backed by every law enforcement agency in America. Meanwhile, they were also becoming more expert.

The authorities employed drug experts, and others who

concentrated on fraud and extortion. There were even shrewd accountants trying to trace Mafia money in European banks and investigating income-tax evasion. It was thought that the operation would take years to complete but there had already been some success: the war was on. In Washington, a gang of drug traffickers was arrested, while in New York 124lbs of heroin was seized. In Ohio, seven men were caught in possession of 100,000 dollar bills.

For years, the Mafia had bled profits from the swollen arteries of a million drug addicts, but in an incredible reversal in the history of organized crime in America, the Mafia turned its back on narcotics in 1970. The reason: sons, daughters and grandchildren of Mafia members were becoming hooked themselves. The Mafia decreed a death sentence for any member caught peddling drugs; a word-of-mouth warning was spread across the United States and the decree extended to those of Italian-American blood, whether they were Mafia members or not.

By totally dropping the narcotics business, the Mafia kissed goodbye to an estimated income of $2 billion a year. But, it was reported that what it was getting in return was an unbelievable deal from the US Government, unlike anything that any other criminal organization could have hoped to engineer. The deal came after word of the halt in dope trafficking was carefully leaked into the United States Justice Department in Washington. A gentleman's agreement was reached that, if the Mafia stayed out of the dope market, the Justice Department, the Federal Bureau of Investigation and government officials would refrain from using the words "Mafia" and "Cosa Nostra" in official speeches, press releases and reports. An order to that effect was circulated in August 1970 by Attorney General John Mitchell with the president's permission. What the Mafia lost from their own ban on narcotics they more than made up for in public relations. It began to bring about a cloak of semi-respectability and a general decrease in the heat being applied by government agencies.

However, the Mafia didn't have it all their own way and despite their cunning PR stunts, which were as devious as their business dealings, bosses did get targeted by rival families. In June 1971, Mafia boss Joe Colombo was gunned down in front of a crowd of 6,000 people. Surgeons fought hard to save his life as he lay in hospital with a bullet in his brain. Colombo, 47, had been at a huge rally of the Italian-American Civil Rights League in New York, attended by top stars including Sophia Loren, Tom Jones and Sammy Davis Jr. At the start of the rally, in an open area known as Columbus Circle, a young black man had strolled up to the platform, pulled out a gun and shot Colombo three times in the head. Panic-stricken men, women and children tried to flee as the police opened fire and killed the man with a hail of bullets. Colombo had formed the civil rights league because he claimed that the use of the words Mafia and Cosa Nostra cast a slur on Americans of Italian descent. His organization picketed the FBI headquarters until the words were dropped from their press releases, as was promised when the Mafia turned their backs on narcotics. He even managed to get the words taken out of the film *The Godfather*, but the FBI maintained that Colombo was the leader of one of the Mafia's top crime families. He was indicted on a charge of controlling a £3 million a year gambling racket.

Following the shooting, the police didn't rule out that Colombo had been attacked in a gangland shooting and they took in three leading Mafia men for questioning, despite a man telephoning a news agency claiming to be from the Black Revolutionary Attack Team. There were fears that the shooting would spark a gang war and the police were concerned about an ensuing bloodbath. Violence was feared on two fronts: a wave of gang wars and an outbreak of race riots.

Colombo continued to fight for his life at the end of June after two bullets were removed from his head during a five-hour operation. He was left in a coma with a 50/50 chance of survival. The man responsible for his condition was Jerome Johnson, who police believed was a hit man hired by a rival gang anxious to take over Colombo's rackets. Those arrested following the shooting included Joseph "Crazy Joe" Gallo and his brother Albert "Kid Blast".

The Gallos and Colombo had been on opposite sides in a gang war 10 years earlier that had cost at least 20 lives. The feud ended when Crazy Joe went to prison for extortion. However, he became a white leader in the Black Power movement and many black men were known to have been linked to his gang. Crazy Joe was freed from jail in February 1971, just a few months before the attack on Colombo, and was thought to have decided to make a move on the Mafia boss. However, a flare-up between Italian-Americans and blacks was also probable.

Another Mafia high-flier, their reputed financial genius Meyer Lansky, faced problems when he was ordered out of Israel in September 1972. The alleged crime syndicate boss was said to be one of the world's richest men and wanted to settle in Israel. He was turned down as a citizen – despite his Jewish connections – because of his "undesirable criminal connections". The high court rejected his appeal against the decision as he had been indicted in America on charges of concealing gambling profits from the tax authorities. Israel was prepared to pay to send the crime boss to any country prepared to have him, but the only likely candidate was the US, where his future home was likely to be a jail cell.

Believed to be worth £100 million, Lansky had arrived in the United States at the age of nine as an impoverished immigrant. But, by his mid-20s he was on the stepladder to Mafia fame. However, due to his Russian-Jewish descent he was denied actual membership of the Mafia, although he still went on to become one of their most influential figures. In the 1920s he became a partner of notorious gang boss "Bugsy" Siegel; in the 1940s he was a victim of a Mafia feud, his associates included Lucky Luciano, Jack "Legs" Diamond, Frankie Costello and Louis Lepke, founder of Murder, Inc. Lansky's main income was from gambling – most of it legal – at a string of casinos stretching along the east coast from New York to Miami.

During a purge against crime in 1950, Lansky served his first and only jail sentence – of three months – for gambling violations.

At the time, a Washington investigating committee claimed that Lansky controlled one of America's two biggest crime syndicates. He then began operations in Cuba and the Bahamas but later turned his attentions towards London. His money was reputed to have been behind the opening of the Colony Club in Berkeley Square in London in 1966. He was also thought to have been involved in several other London clubs. The problem that Lansky faced at the age of 70 was where to take himself when his chosen country didn't want him.

A year later, in April 1973, Vincent Teresa became the most securely guarded man in America when he gave the most astonishing Mafia exposure ever published. Teresa told the truth about the big-time rackets. "Big Vinnie" as he was known was then protected day and night by a team of heavily armed US marshals. He was, at that point, the only high-ranking Mafia boss to have turned informer and his former organization offered £200,000 to anyone who could find him and kill him. Teresa was a top Mafia thief; a mobster and a brutal enforcer who operated at the highest levels of organized crime. Had he not been caught – and had he not been double-crossed – he would have remained a powerful and successful criminal. Instead, over a period of three years, his testimony had been responsible for the indictment or conviction of more than 50 organized crime bosses, including the Mob's biggest moneymaker Meyer Lansky. Teresa contributed information of enormous value to dozens of law enforcement agencies at both the federal and state levels, and he inadvertently became the Mob's most dangerous adversary. Repeated attempts were then made on his life.

It may have seemed remarkable that Teresa turned informer, as for him the act of informing was a violation of a code that he had lived by since childhood. Yet, he talked. The reason was that he had been crossed by his own mob who stole £1.5 million from him and menaced his children. It was this – not the fact that his 20-year sentence was reduced to five years – that made him tell all. His revelations about Mob infiltration of companies, high-ranking criminals in America, crooked casinos, gamblers, fixed horse races, gang wars and Mafia discipline provided the most comprehensive inner look at organized crime ever seen. He had confessed to every type of crime except murder and denied that he had been a "made" member of the Mafia. To be "made" you had to have committed murder. But there was no immunity for murder and Big Vinnie knew and accepted that. He worked with the New England Mafia where he was answerable to only two men, Raymond Patriarca and Enrico "Henry" Tameleo. As their deputy, he supervised the activities of scores of thieves, bookmakers and swindlers, although his connections extended well beyond New England to other parts of the US, the Caribbean and Britain. He was a proficient moneymaker – one of the best the Mob had ever known – and in a lifetime of crime he stole nearly £6 million for himself, which he spent on horses, women and rich living. He stole a further £50 million for his bosses and confederates. Thieves as good as him were held in high regard by the Mafia.

Then, in October 1976 in New York, the mobsters came to town in order to give a big send off to the boss of all bosses. Don Carlo Gambino was dead. The man who had controlled a multimillion-dollar empire of gambling, extortion and rackets, and was the inspiration for Mario Puzo's novel *The Godfather* had died, aged 74, at his mansion in Massapequa, New York. Unlike many of his old colleagues and associates, he died in bed. He was then laid in state in a massive four-room funeral parlour in Brooklyn, where he lay in a large bronze coffin that was luxuriously quilted at a cost of £4,000.

In the days following his death, huge wreaths poured into the funeral home with some resembling small trees. On the day of his funeral, Don Carlo's coffin was taken to the Church of Our Lady of Grace, where an endless line of black Cadillacs glided to a halt, bringing people who perhaps owed their station in life to the man in the coffin. There were those who perhaps even owed him their lives. Strangers were turned away from the church by bouncers; it was definitely a "family" affair. After the service, the coffin was carried back to the hearse, which was followed to the cemetery by three cars carrying the enormous wreaths. Behind them came 13 limousines with the first carrying his daughter and three sons. The 14 sedans that followed carried a number of detectives. The police and FBI agents attended the graveside gathering of the Mafia clan, almost outnumbering the mourners as they took photographs of the underworld elite, noted car numbers and recorded names. It was a magnificent send-off for the man who had landed in America from Sicily as a stowaway 55 years before.

Don Carlo had been New York's Mafia leader for 19 years. As

well as being the head of the five New York Mafia "families" he had also controlled the crime syndicate in five states. He was also the head of the Mafia's 12-member "council", which served as both board of directors for their enormous business empire and the Mafia court that settled internal disputes. It would fall to the council to choose his successor. Police hoped that it would be a businesslike appointment, but feared that it could lead to a bloody gangland battle.

One contender for Don Carlo's throne was his "underboss" Aniello "O'Neill" Dellacroce, who automatically succeeded to the leadership of the Gambino family. Another was Carmine "Lilo" Galante, who had become the head of the Bonanno family when its founder – who once put out a contract on Don Carlo – went into hiding. Galante, who had been linked to at least a dozen murders, was described by the FBI as a "ruthless, fearless, vicious hoodlum".

The organization referred to as the Mafia by police officers, assorted private eyes and tabloid-headline writers across America, was known simply as the Mob. Lawyers and FBI preferred to call it the Nationwide Organized Crime Network. Legally, however, the Mafia didn't actually exist. But a move by a county court in Freehold, New Jersey – in a lethal, bullet-tattooed history of American crime – speculated that proof about the organization would come to light. If the State of New Jersey and indirectly the US government were to win, the decision could blow a hole in the Mafia the size of the Grand Canyon, so it was claimed. It was hoped that its existence could be proved in April 1980 – without guns but by the power of the law.

Freehold was an unlikely setting for such a trial; it would have been like the Krays appearing for trial in a small town in Cornwall. However, five men who stayed distant from each other occupied the first three rows of the left-hand side at the back of the courtroom: all five were accused of being part of the brotherhood. The men included Thomas "Pee Wee" DePhillips, James Vito "V" Montemarano, Andrew Gerardo, Anthony DeVingo and Angelo Carmen Sica. But the star of the show was a local Mafia man, Anthony "Little Pussy" Russo, a New Jersey chieftain and a noted big mouth. It was this big mouth that had got Little Pussy into trouble – and he was poisoned with lead, administered through his head.

The case in Freehold rested on recordings made in restaurants and bars around New Jersey. The threats heard on the tapes were savage. A sample of the stark brutality of threats was revealed by one portion of the tapes. A man named Richard Bohnert had failed to keep up the interest payments on a large sum of money he borrowed from the Mafia. A "persuader" moved in and the following events took place: Bohnert was told that his legs would be broken. He was then threatened that as soon as he left hospital his legs would be broken again and again. In fact, each time he left hospital, his legs would be broken. Later in the conversation, Bohnert is told how his widow would have to fend for their fatherless children. The court case, it was hoped, would provide the US Government with a devastating inroad into the Mafia's defences.

In December 1985, Mafia boss Paul Castellano was gunned

down in a New York street when he and a lieutenant who was driving him were blasted by three gunmen when they drew up outside a Manhattan restaurant. As they stepped out of their black limousine, three men in trench coats emerged from the shadows and fired at least 10 shots into them. Two of the assassins ran off into the evening rush-hour crowds, but the third paused to pump a bullet into the head of 69-year-old Castellano – known as Capo di Tutti Capi, boss of bosses. Castellano was left sprawled on the pavement outside the steak house near the United Nations building and, as head of the Gambino crime family, he had been regarded as the godfather of the Mafia in the US. He was, at that time, on trial accused of ordering 25 murders and carrying out three of the killings himself. Nicknamed Big Paul, Castellano also faced other charges with other Mafia bosses of organizing crime families, robbery and extortion. Police once again feared that the Mafia death would spark a bloody battle for control of the Gambino family.

The Mob paid its final respects to the boss of bosses, Big Paul, on 19th December. He was buried in secret at a cemetery near his New York mansion, but was refused a mass by Cardinal O'Connor, who made it clear that organized crime had no place in the Roman Catholic Church. The Mafia leader's death had brought a sigh of relief to his former underworld colleagues who suspected that had he faced the full trial he would have done a deal with officials in order to save himself from a long sentence.

A year later and the boss of all bosses in Sicily, Luciano Liggio, was caged behind bars as Italy's biggest ever Mafia trial began. A total of 747 mobsters were accused of billion-pound drug running, extortion and other rackets, along with around 100 murders. Behind bars in Palermo, 60-year-old Liggio was said to be the godfather of the island's most powerful and brutal "family", the Corleonesi. He was no stranger to captivity, having previously spent 10 years behind bars, but he was described as a great survivor who had already fought off 12 charges of murder or attempted murder with claims of "insufficient evidence". But now the authorities believed that the marathon trial – expected to last 12 months – would finally destroy Liggio and his henchmen. Two thousand policemen with machine guns patrolled Palermo's streets and marksmen kept watch from the rooftops while hundreds of police officers guarded the concrete courtroom at a cost of £13 million.

Meanwhile, the deaths of Castellano and his henchman, Thomas Bilotti, signalled the birth of the godfather of all godfathers – John Gotti, who faced trial in 1992 for the fourth time as the FBI tried to end his reign of terror. The death of the former head of the Gambino crime family was the end of the chapter in New York's neverending tale of terror, but started the beginning of an even more sinister one with Gotti – the Mafia chief they called the Al Capone of the 1980s – who had won the battle for control of New York's underworld. Over the next few years his crime family, the Gambinos, was to become the most powerful in America. And, a cocky, smirking Gotti would walk free from three trials, earning him the title Teflon Don because nothing would stick.

At Gotti's fourth trial, the most damning evidence came from his own mouth as FBI agents prepared to offer 10 hours of conversations they had taped after bugging the deadly Don's Ravenite Social Club headquarters in Little Italy, New York. On one tape, a furious Gotti decides to make the boss of a rival Greek gang an offer he can't refuse. Gotti is heard growling that he will sever the man's "fucking head" off and, on another tape, bellows: "Any time we got a partner who don't agree with us – we will kill him." Adding weight to the tapes were former Gotti henchmen who had decided to "grass" on him. His former right-hand man Salvatore "Sammy the Bull" Gravano was to testify that Gotti was at the scene of the Castellano killing. This was backed up by two other henchmen who told jurors that Gotti bragged about arranging the former boss's killing.

The revelations sent shock waves around the Big Apple's underworld. The word on the street – despite support for Gotti – was that his luck had run out. And the Gambino family were sizing each other up ready to fill his shoes. His luck did run out and, on 23rd June 1992, mobster John Gotti – who thought he was untouchable – was jailed for the rest of his life. Teflon Don was told there would be no parole. The sentence triggered a riot outside the New York courthouse where 1,000 Gotti supporters, wearing Gotti T-shirts, tried to storm the building. He was convicted of racketeering and five murders. The owner of 2,300 suits had cold-bloodedly murdered his way to the top.

Without the evidence of Sammy Gravano, Gotti would probably have been entitled to keep his Teflon nickname, but it was speculated that he would try to hang on to his powerful position despite being in prison. His chances were described as slim. Gotti had stood in court convinced that no one could touch him. For five years, the ruthless gangster had stuck two manicured fingers up at the law. Gravano's startling revelations put Gotti behind bars for life, without parole, and brought down one of the most powerful Mob families. Sammy Gravano was given a lighter sentence for co-operating with the FBI and was jailed for five years. Today he is a free man. In a book *Underboss: Sammy the Bull Gravano's Story of Life in the Mafia*, he revealed (much like Teresa) the secret inner workings of "Our Thing".

A flamboyant Gotti had brought the real-life Mafia into the public spotlight with himself as its star. A year after becoming the head of New York's most powerful families by ordering the execution of his old boss, he positively courted the media attention heaped upon him. He could barely contain his delight when *Time* magazine put him on its front cover in 1986 with the headline "Crime Boss" and a portrait by pop artist Andy Warhol, which Gotti had framed and hung in the office where he ran his corrupt empire. He was as famous for his sartorial elegance as he was for his ruthlessness and he positively revelled in his status. But, behind the manicures, the coiffured hair and sharp business suits was the mind and body of a man who was dedicated to a life of "family" crime. It was rumoured that when neighbour John Favara accidently killed Gotti's son in a tragic accident – the sons of both Gotti and Favara were friends – Gotti had Favara chainsawed to death. The death of Frank Gotti,

12, had been tragic and Favara was devastated. He received death threats and friends warned him to move away, but he never got the chance. He was clubbed and hustled away into a van by three men. He was never seen again.

In January 1993, another crime boss – also described as the godfather of the godfathers – Salvatore "Toto" Riina, 62, was caught after 23 years on the run. On 15th January, the real Don Corleone was the biggest "fish" to have been caught by Italian police in a trap they had set for him. As head of the feared Corleone clan, Riina was said to have more than 3,000 murders on his bloodstained hands. His ruthless rise to lead all Mafia families in Sicily ended with the longest-ever manhunt and culminated in eight plainclothes police officers stopping a Citroen car near the Sicilian capital of Palermo. The gangster was driving unescorted and unarmed. The net had been closing for three months and police had waited for two days before making their final swoop.

The gangster's face was bloated following plastic surgery but police knew they had their man despite his protestations that they didn't. This man had the ultimate decision on who lived and who died. Following the death of anti-Mafia judge Giovanni Falcone (the death warrant of whom was undoubtedly signed by Toto), the public outrage that ensued urged the Italian Government to put a £15 million bounty on Riina's head. It was assumed that the former boss had escaped to South America or the US to continue running his multimillion-dollar heroin-smuggling operation, but he had remained in Sicily. Since 1969 the police had tried with little success to track him down. He was even tried in his absence for a number of murders and sentenced to life in prison. He became a millionaire in his twenties following vast profits in prostitution, but then entered the drugs world, ruthlessly killing all those who stood in his way. At the time of Riina's arrest, Vincenzo Parisi, the chief of police, said: "This is a death blow for the Mafia. It ends the myth that Riina was uncatchable. The leadership of Cosa Nostra has been decapitated."

But has it … ?

The Richardson Gang

A smaller outfit than the Krays, the might of the Richardson gang was still felt in London's underworld. Their leader, Charles Richardson, 32, was to face 14 charges – some involving fraud and grievous bodily harm – when he appeared at Bow Street Magistrates Court on 1st August 1966. He was arrested during a dawn raid which also saw 10 other men and a woman taken into custody. It was feared by police that witnesses would be intimidated if the magistrate released any of the 11 arrested during the massive swoop. Detective Chief Superintendent Fred Gerrard had objected to any of the 11 receiving bail on the grounds that there were further inquiries to be made and other people still to be arrested. He also told the hearing that there was a threat to witnesses should any of those arrested be granted bail. Richardson's charges included six for causing grievous bodily harm, two of demanding money by force and two of demanding money by menaces. Other charges were an alleged robbery with violence, conspiracy to obtain goods by false pretences, warehouse breaking, theft and assault.

Alongside Richardson was Roy Hall, 25, from Bromley who faced seven charges: five of causing grievous bodily harm, another of demanding money by force and an assault. Derek Mottram, 32, was charged with three counts of causing grievous bodily harm, conspiring to obtain goods by false pretences, demanding money by force and assault. Also accused were Albert Longman, 40, Robert St Leger, 44, Francis Fraser, 24, Thomas Clark, 33, Alfred Berman, 51, Brian Morse, 34, James Kensit, 51, and Jean Richardson, 29. They were remanded in custody. But, despite this, witnesses were issued with police guards when it was learned just how frightened they were to be called in a case in which there had been a history of "extreme violence".

Some witnesses had been the subject of violence already and others were in extreme fear, stated David Hopkin, appearing for the Director of Public Prosecutions at Bow Street Magistrates Court on 9th August 1966. Hopkin applied for a further remand and the 10 men were kept in custody. Jean Richardson was remanded until 10th August when further consideration would be given to her counsel's plea for bail. Richardson, however, was accused of causing grievous bodily harm and of conspiring to obtain goods by false pretences. Hopkin advised the court that there were further inquiries to be made, which would be fairly extensive. The court was also told how Charles Richardson, along with two other men, had tried to bribe one of the witnesses. The accused were also described as a "flight risk": it was known that many of them had already travelled on false passports and the prosecutor was sure that, if bailed, none of them would return to court.

It was revealed in court that Richardson's gang were alleged to have stripped men naked and subjected them to electric-shock treatment, beatings and dousing in baths of cold water at "mock" trials. It was a pattern of violence that had become all too common

AL CAPONE'S COURT SMILE.—Scarface Al Capone (X), the notorious Chicago gangster, smiling broadly during the hearing of vagrancy charges against him in Chicago Municipal Court. He is already under six months' sentence for contempt of Court.

Al Capone Scarface Al Capone (X), the notorious Chicago gangster, smiles broadly during the hearing of vagrancy charges against him in Chicago Municipal Court in March 1931.

Alcatraz Prison on Alcatraz Island, firmly entrenched in the middle of San Francisco Bay, was Al Capone's "home" in the 1930s.

Freddie Foreman Freddie Foreman (fourth from left) outside the Prince of Wales pub after presenting a fundraising cheque to the Mayor of Southwark in August 1967.

In a far cry from his underworld life, Freddie Foreman (centre) poses with Spurs and Wales centre-half Mike England (left) and Spurs and Northern Ireland goalkeeper Pat Jennings at the Royal Garden Hotel Kensington in November 1969.

The Krays Twins Reggie (left) and Ronnie Kray flank their older brother Charlie outside the family home in Valance Road, London, in April 1965.

The Krays were synonymous with organized crime in London's East End in the 1950s and 1960s, including armed robberies, arson, protection rackets, violent assaults and murder.

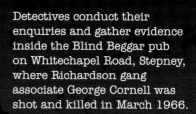

Detectives conduct their enquiries and gather evidence inside the Blind Beggar pub on Whitechapel Road, Stepney, where Richardson gang associate George Cornell was shot and killed in March 1966.

Scene of the amazing charabanc battle between two betting gangs near Ewell. Firearms, axes and hatchets are said to have been used, and seven men were taken to hospital.

Birmingham Boys A feud broke out between rival London and Birmingham betting gangs in June 1921. Firearms, axes and hatchets were said to have been utilized in the affray, which ended with seven men being taken to hospital injured.

A procession of vehicles transports prisoners – held after a bitter battle between rival London and Birmingham gangs the previous week – to their hearings in Epsom.

Jimmy Hoffa In 1964 Jimmy Hoffa (left) was convicted of jury tampering, attempted bribery and fraud and was sentenced to 13 years'. He was eventually imprisoned in 1967 before being released in December 1971, but mystery still surrounds his disappearance in July 1975.

Jack Spot Jack Comer oined his first gang at he age of seven and soon started being called "spotty" because he had a big black mole on his left cheek.

Albert Dimes (below left) outside court with his wife, Rose, in September 1955. Spot credited his barrister, Rose Heilbron, with being "the greatest lawyer in history" after being cleared of the stabbing charge against Dimes.

Following his acquittal over the stabbing of Albert Dimes, Spot "retired" and progressively withdrew from crime. He is pictured here entering bankruptcy court in January 1957.

Frankie Fraser Frankie Fraser first became involved in London's criminal scene during the Second World War and would eventually serve 42 years in more than 20 different prisons around the country.

Frankie Fraser outside the Blind Beggar pub in Whitechapel Road where Ronnie Kray shot and murdered George Cornell, an associate of rival gang the Richardsons, as he was sitting at the bar in March 1966.

Long lost friends! Frankie Fraser greets surviving Kray twin Reggie with a smile at the funeral of Charlie Kray in April 2000.

The faces of East End gangland bosses Kray brothers Ronnie and Reggie as their transport leaves for prison. Both were sentenced to life imprisonment, with a non-parole period of 30 years for the murders of George Cornell and Jack "the Hat" McVitie, the longest sentences ever passed at the Old Bailey for murder.

The team who caught the Krays (left to right): Detective Daphne Robeson; Detective Carole Liston; Detective Janet Adams; Sergeant A Gallacher; Sergeant A Trevette; Commander John du Rose; Superintendent Leonard "Nipper" Read; Inspector Frank Cater; Superintendent Henry Mooney; and Sergeant Algernon Hemmingway.

Reggie Kray pauses at the headstone of his first wife, Frances, during the funeral of his elder brother Charlie at Chingford Cemetery in April 2000. The official verdict was that she committed suicide in 1967, but allegations have since been made that a jealous Ronnie killed her...

The last Kray was laid to rest when Reggie was buried next to his brother at Chingford Mount Cemetery in October 2000.

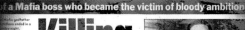

"Big Paul" Castellano succeeded Carlo Gambino as head of the Gambino crime family in 1976. The unsanctioned assassination of Castellano by John Gotti would spark years of animosity between the Gambinos and the other New York crime families.

John Gotti – the Mafia boss nicknamed the Teflon Don because all previous charges had failed to stick and who thought he was untouchable – was jailed for the rest of his life in June 1992 without any possibility of parole. The head of the Gambino family had been found guilty of racketeering and five murders.

Giovanni Brusca – acknowledged to be the Capo di tutti Capo (Boss of Bosses) and believed to be responsible for a spate of bombings and killings across Italy was arrested in May 1996. He murdered the anti-Mafia prosecutor Giovanni Falcone in 1992 and once stated that he had committed between 100 and 200 murders, but was unable to remember the exact number.

Bernardo Provenzano (73), the Mafia's Godfather

The Richardson Gang Charlie Richardson led a group of infamous and sadistic gangsters in London in the 1960s. Also known as the "Torture Gang", their speciality was pinning victims to the floor with six-inch nails and removing the victims' toes with bolt cutters.

GREAT WYRLEY FARM IN A STATE OF SIEGE.

Snapes Farm, the scene of the Great Wyrley outrages in 1903. The occupier is so alarmed by the threatening letters and messages ho has received that he has placed his farmstead in a state of siege. It is barricaded in every direction by corrugated iron sheets, and watched night and day by farmhands, who are fully armed. (Romani.)

Wyrley Gang Snapes Farm was the scene of the Great Wyrley outrages in 1903. The occupier was so alarmed by the threatening letters and messages he had received that he placed his farmstead in a state of siege, barricaded it in every direction by corrugated iron sheets and had it watched 24 hours a day by armed farmhands.

BUTCHER CHARGED WITH GREAT WYRLEY OUTRAGES.

Hollis Morgan, a butcher, was arrested and brought before the magistrates at Wolverhampton yesterday, charged with being concerned in some of the Wyrley mutilations. Morgan, who (marked with a cross) is standing in the dock ...ded by two constables, was remanded till Monday. (Romani.)

Butcher Hollis Morgan, pictured in court in Wolverhampton in September 1907, charged with carrying out some of the Wyrley mutilations.

Alfred Stratton, who spoiled a promising career and killed Mr. and Mrs. Farrow for a few pounds.

Medals won by Alfred Stratton in the Deptford Football League, of which he was once an honoured member.

Albert Stratton, formerly in the Navy. Taken at Devonport. Made a confession in Wandsworth Prison.

Stratton Brothers Brothers Alfred and Albert Stratton were convicted of the murder of Thomas and Anne Farrow during a bungled robbery in 1905 which only netted them around £14. The trial was notable in that they were the first men to be convicted in Great Britain using fingerprint evidence.

The Tottenham Outrage A victim of the Tottenham Outrage in January 1909, PC Tyler's (inset) funeral procession makes its way to Abbey Park Cemetery as thousands pay their respects.

Ralph Joscelyn was an innocent bystander who happened to be in the wrong place at the wrong time. The 10-year-old was tragically shot and killed during the robbery and ensuing chase through the streets of Tottenham.

Police officers flank a suspicious visitor to one of the men accused of the Tottenham Outrage being treated at the Prince of Wales Hospital.

Cleft Chin Murder Wannabe gun moll Elizabeth Jones was accused with US Paratrooper Karl Hulten – a self-proclaimed Chicago gangster – of the murder of taxi driver George Heath in October 1944. Heath was shot dead in his car and his body dumped in a ditch near Staines. Both defendants were found guilty but while Hulten was hanged in March 1945, Jones was reprieved and released from prison nine years later.

Gunther Podola Gunther Podola is arrested at Kensington's Claremont Hotel before being taken to Chelsea police station for questioning over the murder of Detective Sergeant Raymond Purdy in July 1959.

Podola claimed he was beaten up by the police and as a result lost his memory. His trial was notable and controversial because of his defence of amnesia and the use of expert witnesses to determine whether his illness was real.

Shepherd's Bush Murders Police hunt for clues to the identity of the murderers of three London police officers – Detective Sergeant Christopher Head, Detective Constable David Wombwell and Constable Geoffrey Roger Fox – who were shot dead after investigating a battered blue Standard Vanguard estate van, parked in Braybrook Street, with three men sitting inside it.

Harry Roberts (far left), John "Jack" Witney (left) and John Duddy (below) were convicted of the policemens' murder and sentenced to life imprisonment. Public sympathy for the families of the victims resulted in the establishment of the Police Dependants' Trust to assist the welfare of families of British police officers who have died in the line of duty.

in London's underworld. The violence was applied to those who incurred the "displeasure" of company director Charlie Richardson. By this time, there were 15 other men in the dock with the 32-year-old, but only two others were named in the electric-shock treatments, including George Cornell – who had been shot dead in the East End earlier in 1966 – and John West, alias Lawrence "Johnnie" Bradbury, who was at this point appealing against a sentence of death for murder in South Africa.

The 17 accused sat in two rows in a dock specially enlarged for the occasion and enclosed by a barrage of police officers standing shoulder to shoulder. Opening for the prosecution, Edward Cussen said that from 1962 Richardson had carried on numerous activities mainly from 50 New Church Road, Camberwell, a scrap metal works. Cussen talked of a pattern of violence that arose in connection with everyone who had been associated with Richardson in any capacity regarding his activities and also where they incurred his anger. He first detailed the charge against Richardson and Longman, alleging that they demanded £5,000 with menaces from Bernard Wajcenberg.

Just before Christmas 1962, Wajcenberg was invited by Richardson to sell goods on behalf of a firm that was controlled by Richardson and appeared to be operated by two other men including Bradbury. The court was told that, in 1963, Wajcenberg had seen Richardson and his brother Edward – also one of the accused – bring a man named Jack Duval into an office. Wajcenberg noticed that Duval had blood on his face and a black eye. Not long after, Wajcenberg was sent for by Richardson and told he owed the company £5,000 for goods he had sold. He denied the debt but was in no doubt that a demand was being made and it should be provided even though it wasn't owed. He was convinced that he would suffer the same fate as Duval and so he borrowed £1,500 and quickly handed it over. Richardson complimented him on his speedy compliance. Wajcenberg borrowed a further £1,500 and handed that to Longman, but was so frightened that he left for the Continent, where he remained for several months.

Cussen then continued with assault charges against Richardson and Hall, who along with Cornell and Bradbury were accused of causing grievous bodily harm to Bernard Bridges. In 1964, Bridges was a business associate of Duval, who had subsequently left Britain, and so Richardson called Bridges to come and meet with him. Bridges was understandably nervous but felt he had no choice but to go to Camberwell. He was asked to give Duval's whereabouts, but Bridges didn't know. When he stated this, Cornell hit him and he was then beaten by Hall, Richardson and West. He was stripped naked, bound and gagged and tied to a chair. An electric generator was then used to hurt him extremely badly and cruelly, advocated Cussen. Wires from the generator were attached on instruction from Richardson to various parts of his body. Bridges, in his misery, indicated that he wished to talk. The gag was removed and he told Richardson that the only place he could think that Duval might have gone to would be the north of England where he had a former wife. Bridges was then sent to the north to see if he could find

Duval, which he couldn't.

Cussen told the court about Derek Harris, who was also sent for by Richardson in relation to the whereabouts of Duval. Harris, too, was subjected to the electric-shock treatment. There was also an assault on Benjamin Coulston who in January 1965 left his house with his wife and some friends in a van to go to the local pub. He was given information in the pub that his van was being tampered with but when he got outside to investigate was hit on the head and dragged away to another van. He was taken to New Church Road, where he was confronted by Richardson holding a pistol. Also present were Edward Richardson, Frankie Fraser, John West, Derek Mottram and Roy Hall. A man named Rawlings, who was not in court, had also been there as had James Moody and William Stayton, who had been around on and off. Coulston was struck by Fraser with a metal object across the eye. Richardson then ordered that the terrified man should be stripped and searched. Coulston was accused of taking £600 from two gang members. He was then searched and property belonging to him placed on the desk in front of Richardson, who still held the pistol. Coulston underwent a "mock" trial for the missing £600, alleged to have been in connection with a deal over some cigarettes; he was then attacked and beaten by Fraser and Mottram and put into a bath of cold water. Richardson then held a burning electric fire close to his face and his genitals before he was given electric-shock treatment. Despite the fact that Coulston was also assaulted in other ways, he denied any involvement in the missing £600. He was then taken by the gang in the back of the van in which he had arrived, but was surprised to find himself back in Richardson's office as he had heard talk of them dumping him in the river. Back in the office, Richardson gave Coulston some whisky and told him that they had now found out who had defrauded them and they knew it wasn't him. He was given clothing and a plaster to put over his eye. When the gang asked him what he was going to say had happened to him he told them he had "fallen out of a car".

Cyril Green was another victim of the Richardson gang who also suffered an alleged assault. He had upset Cornell who was displeased with the way in which Green had "mismanaged" a bailiff demanding money. Cornell then telephoned Jean Richardson and told her that he was going to give Green treatment and asked for someone to be sent to help him. Hall arrived and seriously assaulted Green by kicking him and inflicting other harm. James Taggart was the next man assaulted; he was beaten severely by Richardson, Clark, Fraser and Berman. He was so terrified that he gave Berman cheques for £1,200 because his company owed around £1,000 to a company that owed Berman £1,200.

Cussen then went on to describe how Arthur Blore had been the victim of grievous bodily harm after he was approached due to his connections to Duval. Blore was asked by Duval to go to New Church Road to assist in clearing up some business matters. When he arrived he witnessed that Duval's face was covered in blood. Blore was hit on the back of the head and while on the floor was kicked in the stomach by three or four people. He was told that, along with Duval, he had robbed Richardson's company Common Markets Ltd of £30,000.

The first witness in the trial was Christopher Glinski, who stated that at the end of 1965 he had been running an export business from Vauxhall Bridge Road. He had an inquiry from a German asking him to export toys from the UK. He bought the toys and paid £350 each to Fraser and Mottram as part of the deal. Subsequently, several men came to his office. "I was frightened. One of the men, Francis Fraser, told me he wanted me to pay the £350 to a Mr Prater instead of to Mottram," he said. But he refused to change the deal and was attacked by four men, including Fraser.

Due to the nature of the attacks, the case was quickly dubbed the "torture" case and two witnesses gave evidence on 3rd October 1966. One described how he was stripped by a group of men, tied up and given electric shocks when being questioned about a £2,500 diamond ring. Another, who was given shocks from an electric "box" while being questioned about a man's whereabouts, added that one of the gang thought there must be something wrong with the box because the witness retained consciousness throughout his torture.

Michael O'Connor, 36, gave evidence against one of the accused, Alfred Berman, on the charge of grievous bodily harm. O'Connor had been taken by Berman and other men in a Cadillac to a building in south London, where he was questioned about a ring alleged to be missing from the home of Berman's wife. O'Connor was stripped and his wrists and ankles bound. Electric wires were attached to him and the best part of a bottle of brandy was poured down his throat. His ear was slashed by one of the men and he received electric shocks. He was also burned on various parts of his body with cigarettes. He started to "pass out" and the next thing he knew he was walking along a street as dawn was breaking. O'Connor was in hospital for nine days following the attack and claimed that the gang had tried to pull his toenails off and pull out his teeth with pliers.

Bernard Bridges then gave evidence against Richardson and Hall. He stated that he had been called to the scrap yard in Camberwell and asked the whereabouts of Duval. When he said he didn't know where his associate was, he had been punched and kicked by Cornell and then Hall had tied him up. He had been stripped down to his vest and shirt and was tied with insulated wire. The electric box was then attached to parts of his body and Bradbury worked the handle of the box in order to give Bridges electric shocks.

On 4th October 1966, police chief Gerald McArthur, in charge of the "torture" case, told the court that witnesses were being interfered with daily in some form or other. He objected to any of the accused being granted bail.

Derek Harris then told the court that he had been stabbed through the foot while the gang discussed dumping his body in the marshes. Because Harris hadn't known the whereabouts of Duval, the wires from the electric box had been connected to his toes and other parts of his body while threats of killing him were made by Richardson. As he was given his clothes back, Richardson had plunged a knife through his left foot and into the floor. There had then been a sudden change in the atmosphere, the 35-year-old told Bow Street Magistrates Court – and Richardson became apologetic and said there had been a mistake. Harris was then given a whisky and £150 and it was arranged for him to be driven home in a car.

On 11th October, the next man in the witness box was businessman Bernard Wajcenberg, who told the court that Richardson had shown him a cabinet full of choppers, hammers and shotguns before threatening him. Wajcenberg, who for safety reasons was allowed to write down his address in court, stated that the incident happened after he had spent five or six hours in Richardson's office, where he was accused of "making inquiries to police officers". Wajcenberg had been forced to borrow £3,000 to pay Richardson money that he didn't owe. He told the court how he'd paid around £20,000 to Richardson for the sale of goods – mainly radios – but had only ever received around £200 in commission.

In the witness box, one of Richardson's business acquaintances, Jack Duval, was asked by John Lloyd-Eley, defending Richardson, if he knew of the Blind Beggar pub. When Duval claimed not to know the pub – which was one of the most notorious hangouts for gangsters in north London in the 1960s – a shout came from one of the accused, perhaps in an attempt to deflect the blame: "Don't tell lies. You know full well you shot him." As well as the charges of causing grievous bodily harm, Richardson was also charged with robbing Duval. It was at the Blind Beggar that George Cornell had been shot in March 1966. Duval also stated in court that he knew of five police officers who were under the control of Richardson and had received money – in the presence of Duval – about five or six times. On one occasion, Duval claimed that £1,000 had been handed over by the gang. Duval also alleged that policemen were given presents in the form of radios, tape recorders and Italian furniture.

When the hearing finished, the "torture" case was sent to the Old Bailey where proceedings opened on 4th April 1967. But, one of the accused, Derek Mottram, 32, was not expected to live should he have to sit in the dock throughout a lengthy case. Mottram had a critical heart disease and stood "in danger of sudden death", his counsel Edward Gardner, QC, told the judge Justice Lawton. A prison doctor, Harold Terry, said it could be hazardous to bring Mottram – by then in hospital at Brixton Prison – to court at all. The judge was due to decide on 5th April as to whether or not the man should have his trial indefinitely adjourned. He also decided that the case should be divided into three separate trials. It was expected that the hearings would last nearly four months and would possibly form one of the longest criminal cases in British history.

When the jury in the trial was formed, it was given around the clock police protection in what was – at the time – the biggest security operation of its kind ever launched by Scotland Yard. Nearly 150 detectives were to take turns in guarding the 12 jurors – 11 men and one woman. The judge also warned the jurors not to speak to anyone about the case, not even the police officers guarding them. The warning came after the jury was sworn in for the beginning of the trial. They then heard the prosecution's case put by Sebag Shaw, QC, who alleged that the chief figure among the accused was Charlie Richardson. The rest of the accused, Shaw stated, were a gang of thugs led by Richardson in his efforts to achieve domination over a group of "tinpot" businessmen. More than 91 people had been turned down for jury service during the course of forming a jury for the trial.

Shaw stated that Richardson had enforced his will over a "rather disreputable business fraternity" by violence and intimidation. The violence, he alleged, had been inflicted "deliberately, cold-bloodedly and with ruthlessness". He added that the trial was not about dishonesty or fraud, but about violence and threats of violence. These were not casual acts of violence, committed in sudden anger or alarm, but vicious and brutal violence, systematically inflicted. When the police had finally caught up with Richardson and his gang, the gangster's policy of violence had been successful for some years. It was so successful, Shaw claimed, that victims of the torture hadn't dared to complain in case worse injuries were inflicted on them and their families. Shaw then held up the electric generator for the jury to see. Two leads had delivered powerful shocks to the victims. Duval came before the jury to tell how on two occasions he had been beaten with golf clubs.

Duval, who was serving a three-year sentence for airline-ticket fraud, was the first witness for the prosecution. He told of an encounter he'd had with the gang in December 1962 when he was taken to their office and struck with golf clubs by Edward Richardson. As he struggled to his feet, bleeding and frightened, he had then been marched to Charlie Richardson's office round the corner, where he was threatened that if he didn't do as he was told he would be beaten again. At the time, Duval was employed by Richardson as a textile buyer for one of his companies. He had had to give an explanation to Richardson as to why a particular part of the business was failing. After being driven home, Duval said he knew he had to leave London as quickly as possible and that he flew back to Italy – where he'd just been on business – and stayed in a flat in Milan until he was better. He was then recalled to London by the gang and ordered to work in a travel business for two agencies. He was then sent back to Italy to start a small company buying stockings, where he was visited by the Richardson brothers and other gang members. Duval claimed that by becoming more and more involved with Richardson he had become more and more frightened. Duval eventually ended up at a friend's house in Brighton, but Richardson tracked him down. He had no choice but to return to London and face his former boss and he was once again beaten with a golf club. After the beating, Duval was taken to a chemist and then bought a new shirt and told in no uncertain terms that he was now on Richardson's payroll. He was "advised" that he should do as he was told.

When Charlie Richardson took to the witness box on 5th May 1967, he protested during his evidence when Sebag Shaw, QC, kept asking him if a prospective witness was alive and well. He told Shaw: "You keep asking me if he is alive and well. It sounds suspicious and may have a bad influence." The judge assured Richardson that all Shaw wanted to know was whether or not the man, Leaworthy, was being called as a witness. But, at that point, neither the defence nor the police had been able to trace him. It also transpired that two other witnesses wanted by the defence had not been found. Richardson spent more than 10 hours in the witness box, repeatedly denying that he had assaulted various men.

But, when Alfred Berman took the stand 10 days later, he told the jury that he had witnessed a beating in Richardson's office. He had walked in to find a man naked and bleeding with a rope around him. Berman said that the naked man was James Taggart and added: "I have never seen such hatred as Charles Richardson showed to Taggart." Berman was the fourth of the accused men to give evidence at the Old Bailey. He stated that Taggart "looked ghastly" and told how his head, ears and eyes were swollen and that there were marks all over his body. Berman said he had remonstrated with Richardson demanding to know what happened, and was told by him that Taggart had taken away another man's liberty and was an informer. Also present, alleged Berman, were Frankie Fraser and Thomas Clark. He also told the court that he saw Richardson kick and punch the naked man while Fraser hit him with pliers. Berman denied punching Taggart and demanding money with menaces.

On 7th June 1967, gang boss Charlie Richardson was found guilty on nine charges in the "torture" trial. Four other men, including his brother, were also convicted on various charges. The trial had lasted 45 days, and the judge ordered that the jurors would continue to receive police protection for some considerable time. They had acquitted Richardson on five counts after three directions from the judge, following nine and a half hours of deliberations. Edward Richardson was found guilty on one count of causing grievous bodily harm and one of assault but was acquitted on five of the eight counts against him. Longman was acquitted of demanding money with menaces – the only charge against him – but was remanded in custody because there were other matters still outstanding. Hall was found guilty on three counts of causing grievous bodily harm and one assault. He was acquitted on three other counts. Fraser was found guilty on two counts of causing grievous bodily harm and one of demanding £1,250 with menaces from Taggart; this was the man who had sparked off the "torture" investigations. Clark was found guilty of demanding money with menaces and of causing Taggart grievous bodily harm. Following the verdicts, Berman and Moody were brought into court and the former was charged with demanding money with menaces from Taggart and causing grievous bodily harm and assault. Moody was charged with causing grievous bodily harm and assault. After hearing some of the evidence read back to them, the jury retired for a further six minutes. Moody was recalled and acquitted but the jury was unable to agree about Berman. The judge then ordered a retrial and both men were remanded in custody.

Charlie Richardson got 25 years in jail as the judge described his "large and disciplined, well-led, well-organized gang". Edward Richardson got 10 years, which was to begin once a five-year sentence he was already serving – for an affray at Smith's Club in Catford – was over. Roy Hall received 10 years behind bars and Thomas Clark got eight years. Throughout the trial, in the basement canteen of the Old Bailey, two women had sat together chain-smoking. They were the wives of two of the convicted men. Maureen Richardson, married to Edward, was the 30-year-old mother of two daughters, who stated that the couple's six-bedroom house in Chislehurst would have to go following her husband's sentencing. One of their daughters who was at public school would have to leave, and she claimed that she would have to sell her car and the furniture. "My husband was a wonderful provider," she said, "but now we will live in poverty, on National Assistance." As well as his sentence, Edward Richardson was ordered to pay up to £2,000 towards the prosecution's case. The other wife was Nula Hall, mother of three young sons, who screamed when her husband Roy was given 10 years. She realized she had a bleak life to look forward to in a two-bedroom council flat in Peckham, south London.

Meanwhile, one woman police officer stood among those praised by the judge at the Old Bailey for their parts in the investigation. Gillian Hoptroff, 22, had played a vital part in the inquiries when she was tasked with gathering evidence that her male peers were unable to do, including shadowing suspects and keeping observation.

Press reports described Charlie Richardson as a "little Caesar" who considered himself above the law and thought that he could rule his cruel empire by brawn and the letting of blood. He was the "brain", or so he thought, said newspaper reports, who became one of the most powerful gang bosses in London by a mixture of force and cunning. The more hoodlums he gathered around him, the happier he was, the papers claimed. As he grew more powerful, he grew evermore cock-sure and was known to have said: "Don't worry about the law. The cops can't touch me." For a long time he was right ... but only because his victims were too terrified to squeal.

The beginning of the end came for Richardson when Londoner Lawrence "Johnnie" Bradbury was sentenced to death in South Africa for the killing of Thomas Waldock, a mining prospector in Johannesburg. In the death cell, before the sentence was commuted to life imprisonment, Bradbury began to talk about the activities of his ex-employer, Charlie Richardson. Scotland Yard was informed of Bradbury's revelations and Detective Chief Superintendent Fred Gerrard and Detective Chief Inspector Arthur Rees were sent to South Africa. They spent weeks interrogating Bradbury and returned to London with some startling information. Chief Superintendent du Rose, then in charge of the central office at Scotland Yard, recruited Gerald McArthur to his team along with Tom Butler and Victor Evans. At one time, there were more than 200 detectives working on the case. Hundreds of statements were taken and witnesses were traced to towns and cities all over the country. And, despite the intense police activity, the gang never heard about the investigation.

When Chief Superintendent du Rose was satisfied there was

sufficient evidence, he organized a master plan to make the arrests. He called 150 police officers to a midnight briefing at Holborn police station and, at 4.00am, teams of police moved off in cars. One by one, the gang were picked up – most of them from their beds. It seemed that wealthy Charlie Richardson, who had amassed a great deal of money in a legitimate scrap business, had returned to the crime of his teenage years because he loved the power it gave him. In his teens, he had run away from an approved school and broke into shops. He had eventually become a legitimate businessman, but the lure of the underworld – the power and the easy money – proved too strong and he became one of the country's most notorious gangland bosses.

After being sent to jail to serve 25 years, Richardson then received another 20 years behind bars – 12 years and eight years respectively – to run concurrently with the 25-year-sentence he had already received when he was found guilty with Longman of conspiring to intimidate jurors in the trial over the Smith's Club affray in 1966 in Catford, southeast London. As soon as he left the dock, his ex-wife Jean – by then married to Peter Coulter from Guildford – stepped into the dock, but was given an absolute discharge. The former Mrs Richardson said: "I am going to start a new life. I have a lot to live down."

In March 1968, Charlie Richardson wanted to remarry and applied to the Home Office to wed South African Jean Lagrange, who had been his former secretary. By this time, he was in Durham Prison and had just had an appeal against his sentence turned down. The application had been made because Richardson was worried about the welfare of his five children. However, Richardson's violent tactics continued in prison and, in April 1968, he was one of those held responsible for riots that broke out; he was the first of the prison's troublemakers to be moved to Parkhurst Prison on the Isle of Wight.

But, despite later settling down and convincing prison authorities he was a model inmate – so much so that he was eventually moved to an open prison and allowed to work as a community worker at Stoke Mandeville Hospital in 1980 – Richardson escaped. The parole board had turned down seven applications by Richardson, without any reasons being given. Lord Longford described Richardson's disappearance stating: "Walking out was a desperate move by a man going off the deep end."

By 26th May 1980 he had been on the run for three days after serving 13 years of his sentence. Lord Longford – a prison reform campaigner – had known Richardson for many years and stated that the former "torture" boss had changed. And, as Richardson hid himself from the authorities, the former employee who had helped to put him behind bars, Lawrence "Johnnie" Bradbury, taunted him from his South African hideout saying: "Come and get me."

Police were concerned that Richardson had already fled the country, but he made a dramatic plea for mercy writing to a friend that: "Fourteen years in incarceration have taken their physical and mental toll on me ... I have become seriously concerned about my progressive mental deterioration." The handwritten letter was then passed to ITV by his friend, Ronnie Munch. Richardson's mother made an appeal on TV for her son to give himself up. Ellen Richardson said on BBC's *Nationwide* that she hoped her son had not "blown his chances" of parole. She thought he had absconded from prison because he was disappointed at being turned down by the parole board for the seventh time. Interestingly, despite the fact that the police couldn't find Richardson, several journalists had managed to catch up with him, but never managed to tell the police in time.

He was eventually traced to Paris, where there was talk of him selling his story for money. This prompted a backlash from some newspapers who didn't agree that their peers were helping the fugitive to remain uncaught. He eventually spent eight months on the run before being recaptured in January 1981. By July 1981, Richardson had moved from the high-security Wandsworth Prison to Lewes in Sussex, and speculation was rife that he would soon be freed on parole. He was released for a few days in October 1983 and eventually walked free from prison on 11th July 1984 after 17 years behind bars. But the release was just temporary. He was finally freed on 26th July and stated that he wanted to give lectures to schools and at youth clubs on the theme: crime doesn't pay. He aimed to set up a registered charity alongside other ex-convicts in order to promote the scheme.

In 2001, Richardson helped the son of a retired City of London police officer to prepare for his A-level exam in media studies. The young student passed with top marks. The film *Charlie* opened in

February 2004, although Richardson didn't want to see the movie about his life. He stated to a national newspaper that he only wanted to think about good things, such as love and awareness. It seemed that the sadistic methods of torture had come to an end for the former London gangland boss who lived a quiet life in the capital.

Incidents

Wyrley Gang

(1903)

It may seem difficult to comprehend, but the age-old crime committed by the Wyrley Gang at the beginning of the 20th century is still very much in existence today. What are the reasons for the mutilation and killing of animals – particularly horses? What are the motivations behind such crimes? Is it for fun or pleasure? Or, does this crime relate back to the historic customs of witchcraft and animal sacrifice?

In 1903, there was a spate of mutilations of horses in Great Wyrley, Staffordshire. Despite the fact that a young solicitor named George Edalji was serving seven years for mutilation crimes, horses were still largely at risk in the county and the atrocity continued long after he was brought to justice. In November 1903, two horses were mutilated in one night with another the following day. The horse found on 5th November that year had been "shockingly" mutilated not 500 yards from the farm of its owner. The district was living in terror and, while the conviction of Edalji had brought some relief, there was now a county-wide panic as to who was carrying out the attacks and why. Had the young solicitor been unjustly accused? It was rumoured that a secret society with a bond of bloodlust was behind the outrageous attacks but, to many, that just sounded totally incredulous.

Next, it was the turn of the area's cattle to come under attack. The police found a partial solution to the mystery via a number of anonymous letters, which they secured from the recipients. Mr Westwood and Mr Hughes both received anonymous letters about the maiming of animals and the latter also received a threat that he would be murdered. Two schoolboys eventually owned up to sending the letters and were remanded for a week. More atrocities were then carried out in the Cleveland district of Yorkshire, where two more horses were maimed in the same way as those in Staffordshire. They were found on West Coatham Farm suffering from severe cuts, believed to have been inflicted overnight, though it was hoped that the animals could be saved.

By February of the following year, the sentence of Edalji was under review by the Home Office and plans to remove his name from the roll of solicitors were deferred until a decision had been reached. That same month in 1904, a farmer's daughter from Great Wyrley, Mary Harvey, was arrested alongside Alfred Loach on a charge of conspiring to send a threatening letter to a Lichfield tradesman, Mr Hall. The couple were remanded on bail and speculation continued as to Edalji's innocence. Edalji, from Birmingham, was the son of the vicar of Great Wyrley and, while he was held in prison, the atrocities continued. In March 1904, there was still no answer as to why the animals were being maimed and it was widely reported that the acts were carried out for no other reasons than "mere bloodlust and love of torture", which managed to raise superstitions and fears amongst the locals – who were accused in the press of not being particularly intelligent.

That same month, two sheep and a lamb belonging to the landlord of the Star Inn in the village were hacked to death. Police arrested a man in connection with the crime, who refused to give any information about himself. Thomas Farrington, a miner, was brought before magistrates for the crime while police investigated yet more cattle maiming. Farrington was found guilty and given three years' imprisonment for the unlawful killing of animals. Then, in south Staffordshire in August 1904, a valuable bay filly was killed in a similar way to the horses in Great Wyrley while, at the same time, a court heard how Edalji had been convicted on evidence that he was prone to wandering the neighbourhood late at night.

That same month, two more horses were found badly mutilated by miners on their way to work at Great Wyrley Colliery. A brown mare was found disembowelled with a 19in wound across the abdomen, while a grey mare, although alive, had a terrible gash to its side. However, a vet deemed that the mare was in terrible agony and she was shot. Both horses had been fine at around midnight when a local man crossed the field in which they grazed, next to a well-used footpath. However, neighbours reported that the horses had been galloping around the field an hour earlier. It was thought that after being attacked, both horses had run wild in the field in agony and their bloodied tracks were found all over the field. The mares belonged to Captain Harrison, a partner at the colliery, who had also lost cattle in the same way in 1903. By this time, George Edalji had been released by order of the home secretary. Although not in the area at the time of the attacks, he was questioned by police. Due to the ongoing atrocities, the police handling of the case came into question, but the home secretary remained adamant that the Staffordshire police were doing all that they could to catch the perpetrator or gang responsible.

By 1907, the attacks and maiming had been ongoing for a number of years and still the police had made no further arrests. Sir Arthur Conan Doyle was convinced that he knew who the criminal was and confirmed it to the police. He gave them a long chain of evidence, which he put together in his best Sherlock Holmes style. However, the authorities failed to arrest the man pinpointed by him and continued to deny Scotland Yard the opportunity to intervene. In August that year, the mystery at Great Wyrley was as great as ever and Conan Doyle reportedly offered his services to the police. However, they denied in the press that he had told them who the culprit was.

Superintendent Bishop of Staffordshire police said: "If Sir Arthur Conan Doyle knows anything at all which will help to throw light on the matter and direct my investigation, I invite him to send such information to me or to the chief constable, or to come here himself and co-operate with us in bringing to justice this common enemy." Meanwhile the maiming continued. It had been established that the criminal was right-handed with an expert knowledge of horses.

In September 1907, police arrested a butcher from Wyrley, Hollis Morgan. He was taken from his work at Horsley Fields just outside Wolverhampton and charged with maiming two horses in August, belonging to Captain Harrison. The news caused great excitement in the local area, especially as a further attack had just taken place. A mare was found at Brewood, some miles from Great Wyrley, suffering from a wound that bore every resemblance to the earlier attacks. The animal was fairly old and quiet and had a wound on one of its hind legs about 4in long and 3in deep. There were also hoof-marks all over the field in which the mare was grazing, suggesting that the attacker had chased the animal; it was the fourth case of injury in the district in less than three weeks. Two attacks were reported earlier in the week in Walsall, while a farmer, John Cartwright, had a grey mare attacked at Hobble End. One farmer was so frightened by anonymous letters he received that he put Snapes Farm, the scene of the first attacks, under siege. The farm was barricaded in every direction by corrugated iron sheets and was watched night and day by armed farmhands.

Hollis Morgan was taken to court on 6th September 1907 charged with maiming a horse on 26th August. When police searched his home, they found a broken pipe stem in the pocket of one of his waistcoats (a broken pipe had been found by the mutilated horse and the mouthpiece could have matched the pipe bowl). With evidence about the pipe also given by May Holding, who visited the prisoner's lodgings on a daily basis to assist the owner of the house in Bridge Street, Morgan was held on remand and taken to the county jail.

When he was brought back to court, his defending counsel had nine witnesses who stated that the accused was at home before and during the attack he was supposed to have committed. The court heard how Morgan had been in Wolverhampton on the night when Captain Harrison's horses were wounded and that the cap and pipe found by police did not belong to him.

The small court was crowded when Morgan faced magistrates at 10.30am on 9th September 1907. Inspector Lewis, giving evidence for the prosecution, admitted when questioned by the defence that the pipe bowl did not fit the stem and that a cap, also found at the scene, did not belong to Morgan. The accused's landlady also stated that she did not believe her lodger had been out on the night in question and that he would not have been able to leave the house without her knowledge. However, Morgan was once again remanded without bail. Meanwhile, May Holding received a threatening anonymous postcard with a Walsall postmark, which was immediately handed over to police.

The next person to receive an anonymous postcard, which was posted in London, was the accused's landlady, Mrs Thornhill. It read, "Mrs Thornhill – Look out for the first of next month. Your time has come. I will strike you down with something as I struck the horse down at Wyrley. The verdict will be willful murder, not half". The writer also embellished the card with various sinister drawings, including a knife attached to a long stick, a heart with a dagger through it and a horse's head with daggers stuck through it.

Detective Inspector Lewis was the next person to receive an

anonymous letter, which was even more violent in its threats than previous correspondence had been. Scrawled in pencil and signed "One of the Gang", the letter was embellished with crude and mysterious designs of human eyes and crossed daggers. The writer declared that members of the gang were in Wolverhampton and were watching the inspector and also stated that: "If Lewis is not done for, Morgan will get convicted." May Holding received a further letter in mid-September, which read: "You be careful. We aren't at this game for nothing. You can give Lewis a hint though. We aren't going to hang around Wyrley for all time. There's other places. Let him keep his silly eyes open." Mrs Thornhill received a further death threat, which stated: "Mrs Thornhill, I'll kill you".

On 15th September 1907, police dropped the charges against Hollis Morgan and he was set free by the court. The case had completely collapsed due to lack of evidence; there was nothing on which a jury could be expected to convict the butcher. Loud cheers and applause were heard throughout the court when Morgan was declared a free man, which rippled through to the crowd gathered outside the courtroom.

The gang was true to their word, however, and threats of maiming were received by the Cornwall Constabulary in Newquay. The letter read: "There are five of us, two here and three more to come. They can have all the horses locked up and guarded if they like. It will be no use, for they are doomed. Edalji is innocent and so is Morgan". Copies of the letter, which also stated that the maiming would start by the end of the week, were transmitted to every police station in

Cornwall, while police did their best to contact as many farmers and animal owners as possible. But, the first animal to suffer was a valuable cob in a Worcestershire village near Halesowen. It was found with a wound 5in long and 4in deep.

Mrs Thornhill and May Holding continued to receive threatening letters. One of the letters referred to "operations" to be carried out in Kent, while another threatened to "break down" Mrs Thornhill's door and "shoot her down". A further letter threatened that another horse in Wyrley would be killed as soon as things "were quiet again". The note also mentioned that the writer was in possession of a bomb and was signed off: "The Secret Wyrley gang of horse-killers". The final note again referred to a bomb and was signed by "The Mysterious Captain". The letters then continued, with Mrs Thornhill receiving yet another note signed by the "Captain of the Secret Wyrley Gang and Clever Horse-Killers". "I want four men," it began, "to join our secret gang. I shall pay them £100 each down and £20 a week after as long as they do not be traitors. All they have got to do is to watch Inspector Campbell and report to me when there is no policemen about." The letter also included further references to bombs and guns. Then things were quiet for a number of years before there was a warning in September 1912, which read:

WARNING NOTICE

There will be another maiming outrage later on in this district by our clever gang, who can do the blue devils down any time when it is wanted. I will tell the blue bottles how the gang is working by my orders. There is one to do the maiming, one to write the warning notices out, and there is (sic) four to watch the blue bottles about day and night time. The maiming outrages started this last time in July last. I have paid the gang £900 to do the blue bottles down because I owe them a grudge.

G H Darby, Captain of the Wyrley Gang,

Headquarters, Market Place, Wyrley

The warning, which was received on 3rd September, was sent to the editor of the Wolverhampton *News and Star*, just a short time before there was another maiming. The victim was a black pony belonging to a local traveller, which was grazing on some waste land at Stowheath Lane between Wolverhampton and Bilston. It had three severe stab wounds under its left shoulder. There was no doubt that the injuries were deliberately inflicted. Police continued to be baffled.

Just a few days later, it was revealed that threatening letters had been sent to Staffordshire's chief constable and the governor of Stafford jail. Police remained unconvinced that the author of the warning notices and the perpetrator of the maiming were working together, or in fact, the same person. Captain Anson of Staffordshire police was of the opinion that there was no connection between the maiming carried out at the beginning of the century and those carried out from 1912 onwards, because the way in which the animals were injured was completely different. By the end of the month, a further warning was sent by the gang and "Captain Darby" stated that a maiming of two horses and a colt had failed because the knife to be used in the attack had broken. He also added that he had bumped into a policeman he knew from Dudley, to whom he paid £100 in gold not to report the gang. He was to pay the policeman £50 a week for as long as he remained undetected. The policeman was also supposed to have received a death threat should he turn the man in to the authorities.

For three years, "Captain Darby" remained silent and then, in September 1915, he reappeared when a pony in Darlaston was badly injured. However, he'd sent a note to a local newspaper the previous year to say that there would be no maiming until after the war (the First World War 1914–18). And, following the maiming of the pony, he sent a letter to a Wolverhampton newspaper stating that if certain policemen didn't leave the force immediately then he would turn to murder, rather than severely injuring animals. At about the same time as the postcard was received, a bay gelding was found severely wounded between West Bromwich and Wednesbury with a cut 15in long and 3.5in deep.

In 1919, the man describing himself as the captain of the Wyrley gang notified local newspapers that his horse-maiming activities would resume. He stated that the next attack would take place in West Bromwich, despite the fact that nearly all the gang was reportedly killed during fighting in France. Calling himself Count von Darby, the gang leader's motives for the attacks remained unclear, but newspapers hinted at a feud against the police. One newspaper reported: "Seeing that all the horses have usually been maimed about the time of the new moon, it is thought that the outrages are the work of a madman." By the end of September 1919, "Count von G H Darbyathe" claimed to have six men from Berlin. He warned that as no policemen had yet left the force as instructed, there would be a maiming outrage at Hill Top.

For four years, with no further attacks, people living in the Black Country were hoping that the notorious Darby was dead. However, they were dismayed to find in 1923 that he was up to his old tricks and threatening to mutilate animals once again. Chief Inspector Cooke of Walsall police said that the letter bore little resemblance to earlier threatening notes. The handwriting differed substantially and was much larger than in the originals. But, police quietly prepared for eventualities because the home secretary was threatened with being shot dead if he did not leave his job within one month.

In October 1934, 57-year-old Enoch Albert Knowles from Darlaston was charged with "sending letters threatening to murder and sending offensive communications through the post". Ernest Brown, for the prosecution, talked of threatening letters having been sent for more than 30 years. Knowles, despite being a nasty pest and a menace, had gone undetected for more than three decades. He was committed to the Stafford Assizes on charges relating to the letters sent and was sentenced to three years in jail on 6th November. As to the identity of the attacker, no trace was ever found of him or his gang.

Animal mutilation continues unabated today. But why? Is it because the perpetrators suffered child detachment issues in early life and have no empathy for the creatures they cruelly torture, or is it possible that they are getting back at society for some long-held grudge? There are those who suspect that witchcraft or a satanic cult is involved, but many mutilated animals seem to have been cut with "surgical precision". There are also those who believe that aliens have a part to play in the mutilation of animals, but the truth is that there is no real evidence to support any of the theories offered.

The Stratton Brothers

(1905)

"Under circumstances dramatic enough to be conceived by Poe or De Quincey," the newspaper article began, "three masked men callously murdered an old man and inflicted terrible injuries on his wife in Deptford High Street."

It was 27th March 1905, and Tom Farrow and his wife Anne, the guardians of a prosperous paint shop, were attacked for the week's takings. An errand boy who arrived for work at 8.00am in the morning found that the red shutters of the shop were still up and the shop was quiet. He shook the door but was unable to open it. He then peered through the keyhole and was frightened by the silence that greeted him. He called a neighbour and together they forced their way in around the back of the shop. They entered the sitting room and found the manager of the shop dead on the floor. His wife was found unconscious upstairs. When police arrived on the scene, they found three masks – made from stockings – carelessly thrown aside along with fingerprints, pointing to the fact that three men had been involved. Anne Farrow – from her hospital bed – was able to whisper to the police what had happened during the attack.

At about 6.00am, just as the high street began to show signs of life, three men approached the paint shop. As two hung back, one knocked on the door and Tom Farrow, believing it to be an early customer, was only partially dressed as he opened the door. The stranger apologized to the manager for the early call and asked to be supplied with some painter's materials. As Farrow opened the door wider for the man to come inside, he was struck hard and fast and quickly fell to the floor. The two other men then stepped into the shop and all three put on masks. They ransacked the shop and went through to the sitting room behind, where they were followed by a staggering Farrow. There was a scuffle and the elderly man fell to the floor again in his attempts to protect the owner's goods, but his wife had heard the commotion and called out. One of the men had then raced upstairs and struck Anne Farrow as she sat in bed. The men continued their search of the premises before two removed their masks and walked out of the shop. The third waited for a moment before shutting the door on its spring lock.

One of the attackers was aged about 25 to 30 years old and about 5ft 7in tall. He had a round face, a dark moustache and wore a hard felt hat and a blue serge jacket with the collar turned up. The second suspect was described as about 24 years old and around 5ft 5in in height, with light brown hair. He was dressed in a shabby, brown jacket suit with a grey cap and brown boots. There was no witness sighting of the third man. The murderers had a two-hour head start on the police and for two days managed to evade arrest. But, police were watching at least one house in Deptford and arrests were said to be imminent. The stockings were the chief clue in the case, as they were believed to have been worn previously.

Two of the men had also been spotted by the milkman, Jennings, and his apprentice, Edward Russell, 11, who witnessed their departure from the shop. Russell was able to give a graphic account of the men's getaway. Another witness, a lady from Deptford Green, told police how a few nights earlier, she had been in the shop talking to Tom Farrow when two men had entered the premises and asked to buy paint. Only one of the men had spoken; the other had stood with his back to the witness while staring intently into the sitting room beyond the shop. By the end of the month, the murderers were still in hiding, but Anne Farrow was beginning to make a little progress in her recovery.

It transpired that the masks the killers wore were made from the victim's own stockings, which they had found downstairs at the scene of the murder. As it was unusual in 1905 for criminals in Britain to use stocking masks – which was far more likely in the United States – there was some speculation that the murderers were American. The inquest into 73-year-old Tom Farrow's death was opened on 30th March at Deptford Congregational Hall. It was announced that Anne Farrow had also died, but this was proved to be an error due to someone misreading a telegram. However, she did contract pneumonia and it was not expected that she would live. On 3rd April 1905, two men were arrested and charged with the crime.

Brothers Alfred and Albert Stratton, aged 22 and 20 respectively, were taken to Greenwich Police Court. Alfred had been arrested at the King of Prussia pub in Deptford, while his younger brother was picked up walking along the high street. An identity parade was held, but neither brother was picked out of the 16-strong line-up by the milkman or his young apprentice, although Helen Stanton, a witness in the case, picked out Alfred Stratton. The brothers were held on remand. A week later, the Treasury postponed the opening of their case as Sir Thomas Stevenson, an expert for the Home Office, had not concluded his examination of certain items of clothing.

The brothers were brought before the new Tower Bridge Police Court on 18th April 1905. The prosecutor, Muir, stated that Alfred Stratton had quarrelled with the girl he lived with at Brookmill Street, Deptford, on the night before the murder. In the middle of the night, there was a tap on the window and Stratton left the house to talk to his brother Albert. A short while later, Alfred left the house and, when he returned, after the time the murder had been committed, he smelt of paraffin. The girl with whom he consorted mentioned the smell to him, but he ignored her remark.

At Albert Stratton's house, masks made from stockings were found resembling those at the paint shop. In addition, Muir stated to the court that a print found on the cash box from the Farrows' sitting room matched the right thumbprint of Alfred Stratton. His girlfriend also noticed that, after a description of the murderer's clothes was published in the press, Alfred disposed of a brown coat and blackened his brown boots. When the brothers returned to the hearing on 19th April, there were some intensely dramatic scenes. Albert Stratton's landlady had found masks under a mattress and was cross-examined by Alfred Stratton. However, the brothers' casual approach soon came to an end when their mother entered the witness box. All three were in tears, although Mrs Stratton didn't have much to add to the case. Another witness, the landlord of the house where Alfred lodged, remembered the night before the murder when Albert had tapped on the window.

The inquiry was adjourned. Then on 20th April the two brothers, without a sign of apprehension or remorse, heard a verdict of "willful murder" returned against them by the coroner's jury. Callous and defiant, they burst into scornful laughter when the foreman announced the result of the jury's brief deliberation (it had taken 15 minutes), and they walked out of the courtroom with as much bravado as they'd had when they walked in. The brothers had sat in court whistling popular tunes and stamping their feet on the floor rather than taking the case seriously. Robbery had been the motive for the attack, but there was no evidence to suggest that a third man had been present at all. A vast crowd had assembled to see the two men led away in handcuffs to Brixton Prison.

However, the fingerprint evidence was challenged in the closing stages of the inquiry. The defence, Budden, asked for the case to be postponed while he brought in an expert, but he then declined to bring in his expert and the value of the fingerprint evidence was brought against Alfred Stratton at the Old Bailey in May 1905. Then, on 5th May, in a dramatic twist, there was a "shudder" of surprise in the public gallery when it was raised that Albert Stratton had accused his elder brother of the crime. His accusation was, in part, a confession with the counsel's comment on this voluntary statement giving overwhelming testimony of Albert's guilt, without being evidence against him. Opening counsel also stated that the motive for the crime was undoubtedly robbery and that just £13 had been taken.

As Judge Channell took his seat on the bench, the public noted in grim detail that he carried the black cap in his hand. "Not guilty", pleaded the two prisoners looking straight at the judge. Alfred sat bolt upright and impassive, while Albert leaned back in the dock and occasionally closed his eyes. The woman living with Alfred had remarked about the description of the two men given in the newspapers following the murder. "How like you it is," she had said to Alfred. When Albert's statement that his brother had committed the crime was read, the two brothers were careful not to look at each other. Albert watched the effect of his statement on the jury, while Alfred looked with half-shut eyes at the judge. The trial lasted just two days and the jury returned a verdict of guilty for the deaths of Tom Farrow and his wife Anne.

Judge Channell, assuming the black cap of doom, pronounced a capital sentence. He concluded his summing-up with the following: "The sentence of the court upon each of you is that you be taken from hence to the place from whence you came, and there you be hanged by the neck until you are dead, and may the Lord have mercy on your souls." The brothers had stood to hear their fate and looked blankly ahead. They were then removed from the dock to be taken to Wandsworth Prison, where they were to be given three weeks to make the best use of the time that remained to them. Alfred Stratton had fought hard for his life while in the witness box. His defence, Rooth, argued that the case rested on theory and surmise, but the jury disagreed.

It was the fingerprint evidence that brought the brothers to justice, and despite arguments by the defence that it was not an exact science – the technology was still in its infancy – the Home Office believed that fingerprinting was a reliable new way of identifying the perpetrators of crime. In fact, 5,000 cases had been proved by fingerprint evidence during 1904 alone. It had been proved that the minute skin markings on the tips of the fingers are never exactly the same in any two individuals on all eight fingers and two thumbs.

The skin of the fingers is really two skins – the inner, true skin, and the outer epidermis. This inner skin is covered with little papillae like minute sugar-loaves, which contain the sensory nerves and blood vessels. Over these is an outer skin which, though continually worn away and renewed, takes its markings from these papillae that it covers, and which do not change. The impressions are divided into four main groups including loops, arches, whorls and composites, which all have subdivisions. This means that the number of ridges between various characteristic points is always the same. In the early 1900s, fingerprinting was becoming damning evidence for criminals. If criminals didn't want to remove the ridges – which would have caused the loss of the sense of touch – then they began covering their fingertips with thin Indian rubber, goldbeater's skin, or silk finger-stalls. Some would wear kid gloves.

Meanwhile, Alfred and Albert were kept separate at Wandsworth Prison, where both had put on weight since their conviction. They were allowed four cigarettes each a day. It was also becoming clear that a number of burglaries carried out in the Deptford area had the hallmarks of the Stratton brothers. The brothers were allowed to see their mother and friends for the last time just a few days before their executions. At 9.00am on 23rd May 1905, Alfred and Albert Stratton faced the gallows side by side. To the public, a formal announcement was posted on the gates of the jail to signal the end of their nefarious careers.

The Tottenham Outrage

(1909)

The Tottenham Outrage happened on 23rd January 1909 when two Bolsheviks of Russian origin – Paul Hefeld, 23, and Jacob Lepidus, 25 – attempted an armed robbery of Schnurmann's Rubber Company in Chestnut Road, Tottenham. In an attempt to get away, the two gangsters began a long chase that involved shooting. Two people, PC William Tyler and 10-year-old Ralph Joscelyn, were killed when they were caught in the crossfire. Except for a few pounds found in the pockets of Hefeld and Lepidus, the £30 they stole from the factory before terrorizing the neighbourhood for two hours remained unfound.

Before the robbery, Hefeld had worked at Schnurmann for a short time, where he quickly learned that the weekly collection of wages took place on Saturday mornings. The wages clerk, 17-year-old Albert Keyworth, was taken by car to the bank in south Hackney, London, to collect around £80. Hefeld and Lepidus were both armed and waiting on Saturday 23rd January as Keyworth got out of the car on his return from the bank. Lepidus grabbed the teenager and tried to snatch the money, but he was restrained by factory chauffeur Joseph Wilson. At this point, Hefeld fired at Wilson, but the man's heavy clothing meant that none of the bullets penetrated his body. Lepidus then fired at the wages clerk and missed. The shots alerted two police officers from the nearby Tottenham police station, who ran towards the firing.

They arrived at the factory to find George Smith, a local man, beating Lepidus. Smith was shot twice by Hefeld, and the two robbers ran from the scene pursued on foot by Constables Tyler and Newman, with Wilson following in his car. Other officers began to join the chase as did members of the public – many of whom had weapons from their army days – and the two fugitives began firing indiscriminately at those pursuing them. As Wilson, now with Constable Newman on board, tried to run at the men in his car, the two robbers fired a hail of bullets at their pursuers and 10-year-old Ralph Joscelyn was hit by a stray bullet. He died in the arms of a bystander before he could be taken to hospital.

In the chaos, the car crashed. Another constable borrowed a revolver from a member of the public, but his shots missed the two fleeing men and the chase moved on to Tottenham Marshes. Constables Tyler and Newman then ran across waste ground in an attempt to cut off the two men. Tyler came face to face with Hefeld, who calmly shot the officer in the head. He was admitted to hospital but died within a few minutes.

Hefeld and Lepidus were being cornered by the growing numbers of officers who had joined the chase, and they wounded a number of bystanders in their attempt to stay uncaught. They eventually hijacked a tram bound for Leyton and one passenger was shot in the throat while several others escaped. They then jumped off the tram and stole a milk cart after shooting its driver in the chest and arm. The cart crashed when it failed to negotiate a bend in the road; the men then hijacked another horse and cart. The two men were still firing at those chasing them when they crashed the second cart. As Lepidus climbed over a high fence, Hefeld was left behind with a crowd closing in on him. He shot himself in the right eye, but survived and was taken to hospital. Lepidus took refuge in a family's cottage – while police rescued children from the property – in Hale End Road. The fugitive appeared at a front bedroom window and was driven back by gunfire from police and civilians alike. Officers eventually broke into the bedroom after firing shots. They heard a shot from inside the room and opened the door to find Lepidus dead. He had shot himself. As well as two fatalities and a dead gunman, there were around 25 others who were injured in the two-hour chase that covered just over six miles.

The inquiry into the deaths of Constable Tyler and Ralph Joscelyn was opened by Forbes, the coroner, on 27th January 1909. At the inquest into Lepidus's death, Constable Newman told how Constable Tyler had met his death. He and Tyler had pursued the men across a piece of waste land into Dowsett Road, Tottenham, and came up to them near the dust destructor. Tyler had shouted to the men: "Come on. Give in – the game's up", but Hefeld deliberately aimed at the officer and fired. Tyler fell to the ground and Newman went to his colleague, who he found lying on his face with a bullet wound in his head. Medical evidence was heard before the jury returned their verdict, expressing their sympathy for Tyler's widow and commending the police officers and public for their bravery. The coroner, in an unusual move, described to the inquiry how "two alien thieves of desperate character created a scene of terror on Saturday afternoon without parallel in this country, and it must be God's mercy that they did not succeed in dealing out death on an even more wholesale scale." The Metropolitan police issued the following announcement on 29th January 1909:

Tottenham Heroes

The King's Message to Police and Sympathy with Dead Officer's Widow

The Commissioner is commanded to convey to the police officers engaged in the tragedy at Tottenham the King's high appreciation of their gallant conduct. His Majesty also directs that the expression of his sincere sympathy may be communicated to the widow and family of police constable Tyler.

The internments of police constable Tyler and the lad, Ralph Joscelyn, who were murdered in the Tottenham shooting affray on Saturday will take place in Abney Park Cemetery, Stoke Newington, today.

The procession will leave Mrs Tyler's house, in Arnold Road, Tottenham at two o'clock, Mr Herbert Samuel, Under-Secretary of State, will represent the Home Office.

Jacob, the dead Anarchist, whose funeral was reported as having taken place yesterday, will probably be buried this afternoon. The fund for Tyler's widow yesterday totaled £369. Half of the proceeds of the Tottenham Town Band's collection at the Tottenham Hotspur v. Hull football match tomorrow is to go to the fund, and the Chief

Commissioner of Police has given his patronage to a mammoth carnival to be held at the Empress Roller-Skating Rink, Earl's Court, on Friday next, for the same object.

Tyler received a hero's funeral attended by Sir Edward Henry, the commissioner of police, which saw the streets lined with around 500,000 people eager to watch the procession. There was a widespread demonstration of deep public sorrow on the day of the funerals. Ralph Joscelyn was buried at the same time, just a few yards away from the police constable, and there were many wreaths for the victims. Houses kept their blinds drawn, shops were closed and black shutters were put up as a sign of mourning.

The jury's verdict into the deaths of the two victims, man and boy, on 2nd February 1909 said that: "It is an inconceivable scandal that any Government should allow these criminal aliens to find a footing in this country, and we earnestly beseech the Government to take such steps as may remove from Great Britain the odium and stigma of being the last refuge of these criminal desperadoes of the Continent." The jury expressed their outrage at the conditions that had brought about the deaths of the two victims and returned a verdict of murder against Hefeld for the death of William Tyler and murder against Hefeld and the late Jacob for the death of 10-year-old Ralph. Hefeld was then committed for trial on the coroner's warrant. The coroner then complimented the courage of all who had taken part in the chase. Mrs Tyler's fund had, by this time, risen to £1,055, which was announced as sufficient by Sir Albert de Rutzen on behalf of the fund.

Paul Hefeld died in the Prince of Wales General Hospital, Tottenham on 12th February. His condition had become serious just a few days before, but a critical operation had weakened the gunman. The Tottenham Outrage fund was distributed to around 42 civilians who took part in the pursuit, with awards ranging from £1 to £100. Amounts between £1 and £10 were also given to 27 police officers for their parts in the chase and apprehension of the perpetrators.

The "Cleft Chin" Murder

(1944)

A man robbed of almost every clue to his identity was found shot dead in a ditch at Knoll Green, Staines in October 1944. Scotland Yard combed laundries in order to trace a laundry mark – 202 or 302 – found on his handkerchief, and black ink marks, E 83 (81) and IM 202/468, which were found on his underwear. Wheel marks from a car were found near the ditch. The dead man was described as aged between 40 and 45, with dark-brown hair, which was curly and well greased. A patch of skin disease was in the process of healing behind the victim's right ear and he had ink stains on the fingers of his right hand. The man was well dressed in utility clothing, including a navy-blue overcoat, grey chalk-striped suit, with a blue shirt, tie and socks. He had been shot in the back.

The man was identified on 9th October as George Heath, 35, a taxi driver from Kennington Park Road, southeast London. It was believed he may have upset an inkwell as he fell from his desk, and the theory was supported by evidence that appeared to indicate that the man was murdered in a different location to the one in which he was found. Police believed that he had been taken to Staines, in Middlesex, by car. At that point, no one had come forward, despite an appeal for anyone who had heard shooting in the early hours on the day of the murder.

An American soldier was the first to be interviewed over the case of the man with the cleft chin. Heath's car – a Ford V8 – was found in the Fulham area following the murder, while an assault summons – Gill versus Heath – was found to involve the dead man and the landlord of a public house, William Gill. The incident had taken place when a barmaid working for Gill had asked the landlord to accompany her to her lodgings as she wanted to avoid George Heath. The dead man's defence was that Gill had struck him first, knocking him down some basement steps before the landlord's dog was let loose on him.

The police retrieved the revolver that had been used to shoot Heath on 13th October 1944 and an arrest appeared imminent. The victim's death was the sixteenth murder since 1st September earlier that year, and nightclubs in London's Piccadilly square mile vowed not to use freelance drivers to pick up their patrons in the early hours of the morning. One nightclub owner told the newspapers that: "After this case, we are having regular firms only here as a safeguard."

The American soldier, Private Karl G Hulten of Boston, Massachusetts, appeared before magistrates at Feltham, Middlesex on 15th November 1944 charged with the murder of George Heath. In addition, Elizabeth Jones, an 18-year-old blonde dancer, was to appear on remand the following day charged with being concerned with another person in the murder of the victim. The US Army authorities announced that Hulten had been charged with the murder but that he would not be tried by court martial until the case against Jones had been concluded.

It was the first time that a British civilian and an American serviceman had been concerned in a capital charge, and British civil and American military authorities worked together to work out the issues raised by the unusual situation. Then, on 16th November 1944, the case made legal history when the American serviceman and the British civilian were brought together in a British court, charged jointly with murder. At Feltham Magistrates Court, Hulten, 22, and Jones, from Hammersmith, were charged with being concerned together in the murder of George Heath, known as the man with the cleft chin. Without any evidence being given, both were remanded.

On 27th November, Morgan, for the prosecution, demonstrated how Heath was killed by a passenger sitting behind his seat in the taxi. He stated that the killing was: "A deliberate, cold-blooded act." Jones was described in court as a striptease artist at a nightclub, who was married although her husband was serving abroad. She met Hulten in Hammersmith, where the paratrooper had been frequenting nightclubs, cafes and bars, and the two soon hooked up and became lovers. According to a statement by Jones, she and Hulten – who claimed to be both an officer and a Chicago gangster – left her room on 6th October with the avowed intention of stopping a taxi and robbing the driver.

In Kensington, opposite Cadby Hall, Jones stopped the taxi driven by Heath who agreed to drive the couple to the end of King's Road, Hammersmith, for 10 s. (50 pence). At the end of

Chiswick Road, Hulten told him to stop and Heath then leant over from his seat to open the rear door for Jones. While he was doing so, he was shot in the back, said the prosecution. The bullet then struck the door and ricocheted on to the dashboard. Dr Teare, the prosecution expert, surmised that the victim was shot by someone sitting behind him and that he would have died within 15 minutes of being shot. He was then pushed into the passenger seat and Hulten took Heath's place at the wheel.

While Heath was dying, Jones rifled through the victim's pockets and robbed him of everything he had of value, which amounted to £4 in notes in his wallet, about £1 in change from his pockets, a watch and a pen. Once the man was dead, the couple dumped him in a quiet spot before driving back to London in the victim's car. They threw the bullet from the car on the way back to the city and abandoned his car in Fulham after carefully wiping their prints from the vehicle. That night, the couple stayed together at the girl's room.

When the case came to trial at the Old Bailey, there was a rush for tickets in the "cleft chin" murder. However, the gallery of the court was closed to the public and there were only 40 seats available, which were given on a first come, first served basis. A spokesperson for the Old Bailey confirmed that the court never reserved seats for cases and certainly never sold tickets for entry.

On 17th January 1945, a deathly pale girl sat drooping and motionless in a brightly lit court at the Old Bailey while counsel read a statement that she was alleged to have made to the American paratrooper. It read: "I would like to do something exciting – like becoming a gun moll, like they do in the States." While there was a rustle in the courtroom to hear the statement, said to have been made by Hulten about small-town Welsh girl, Jones, the accused, who was once described as "a lovely blonde" but now "worn out, sick and broken" seemingly showed no interest in her fate. All through that day, she sat motionless.

A witness, Lenny Bexley, a diminutive man who went to the "dogs" with Hulten and Jones on the day following the shooting, went into the box to describe the progress of the friendship of the couple. Then the revolver used in the shooting was brought up in court and Bexley confirmed that Hulten had been immensely proud of the gun and had showed it to him three times. The accused had even laid it on the table in a Hammersmith cafe when he sold to Bexley the pen he had taken from the victim. The next witness was Edith Evans from King Street, Hammersmith, who was Jones' landlady. She gave evidence about the comings and goings at her home in the fateful week that Heath was shot. Then Maurice Levine, a Hammersmith barber, took the stand to describe how he had come to buy the victim's watch from Hulten on the morning following Heath's death. The next witness was Detective Inspector Percy Reed, who had a fierce technical discussion with counsel about the revolver.

Lieutenant de Mott, an American Army CID agent, was put under a close cross-examination by Hulten's counsel, John Maude, for two days in succession. With the judge intervening frequently and

Maude repeatedly complaining that he could not hear the witness, De Mott clung rigidly to his testimony. Statements alleged to have been made by Hulten were read, in which the accused said that he had held the gun to his chest when Heath stopped the car, and had intended to shoot straight through the car, when suddenly – just as he pulled the trigger – Heath heaved upwards and sideways in the driving seat in an attempt to open the rear door on the opposite side. The fact that this statement indicated the possibility of an accidental shooting was stressed at great length by the defence. Parts of Hulten's statements were suppressed by general consent, but Maude later recalled De Mott to talk about the one sentence not previously mentioned: that during a conversation between Hulten and Jones, the girl had expressed her wish to do "something exciting" and that she wanted to be a gun moll ... something that the self-proclaimed gangster had obviously been happy to oblige.

Jones' mother, Nellie Baker, was in Court 1 to see her daughter stand trial accused of murder. Dressed in black, Baker sat with her husband in the public seats at the right of the dock and gazed pitifully at her daughter. She told reporters outside the court that: "It is so long since I saw her. I did so much want just one little word," which the judge had refused earlier that day in court. In the dock, a policewoman stood between the frail, grey-coated girl and Hulten, short and thick-set, with a faint smile half raising his heavy features. Hulten had been seen doodling in court and it was soon apparent that this was an important point in the case.

Maude fought for two and a half hours to prove that two

incriminating statements made by Hulten were inadmissible in an English court. He tried to show that they had been obtained under pressure over an unduly long period. However, the prosecution claimed that the accused's doodling between questions and answers were what prolonged the interview taken by De Mott in the presence of two British detectives. Maude then recalled De Mott yet again in order to question him about the methods used in the interview. But the American Army CID agent quietly refuted any charges of irregularity.

It was 18th January 1945 when Jones hesitantly entered the witness box to tell her side of the story. She faced a jury accused of murdering Heath jointly with Hulten. A hush fell on the courtroom at 2.16pm as she quietly told the events of her 18 years. She told the court how, on the day she married her husband, paratrooper Lance-Bombardier Stanley Jones, the couple argued and she had left him at once (he was reported missing, believed killed in Arnhem on the day that the accused was charged). With one hand in the pocket of her shabby grey coat, buttoned high to the neck, Jones stood swaying slightly in the dock. Haltingly, and in a scarcely audible undertone – but with a marked American accent – she began to give the jury an insight into her unhappy life.

She told how she had been born in Wales, but had moved with her family to Canada at the age of three, where they had lived for five years. When Jones was 13 years old, the father that she loved deeply was called up and she told how she had never been happy again. The family had returned to Wales by this time, and on three occasions she tried to leave home in order to return to her father. She told how, at the age of 16, she married Lance-Bombardier Jones, who struck her on the first night of their marriage, and how she had never lived with him. With continued requests from the judge and jury to speak louder, the girl in the dock who had tearfully described herself to policeman as "a bad girl" due to her drinking so much for her age, told how she had come to London in January 1943, just two months after her marriage. She had worked as a barmaid, an usherette and a cafe waitress, but in April had realized her ambition and found a job as a dancer – a striptease artist in a West End nightclub. Late in 1943, her job as a dancer was over and she lived on the small army allowance that she received from her husband, from whom she had never formally separated. She was asked by her defence counsel, Casswell, if she had ever been a prostitute. She breathed sharply and brushed her eyes with the back of her hand before answering loudly: "No, sir."

Questions then turned to the night that George Heath was murdered and the story of the man who she knew as "Ricky", who sat in the dock staring hard at her. "I thought he was a gentleman," she said bitterly of Karl Hulten. She had allegedly told Hulten that she wanted to do something dangerous, such as flying over Germany, and it was at this point that "Ricky" told her he was a gunman. She told the court that when they got into Heath's car she thought they were going home, but she was too afraid of the American to question him. After Hulten had asked the driver to slow down, she saw the gun in his hand, and when the car stopped she heard a shot. She said how she had been ordered to go through the dying man's pockets and that she refused, but Hulten had indicated with the revolver that she should do what he said. He allegedly told Jones that: "I will do the same to you if you don't go through his pockets." Jones described that while she was looking through the victim's pockets, he was breathing heavily. She did not help Hulten drag Heath into the ditch. Back in Jones' room she told Hulten that he had committed cold-blooded murder. When she asked him why he'd done it, the American had said: "People in my profession are used to things like that. I always get people who inform against me first." Jones declared that when she went on the car journey, she did not know that Hulten intended to rob the driver. However, when Hulten went into the witness box, it was a very different story.

The American paratrooper denied that he had ever been a Chicago gunman; he said he had never even been to the city. The accused also denied that he had ever told Jones that he was a gangster in America and had been running a similar racket in the UK. Asked to explain the events leading up to Heath's death, Hulten said: "We had decided to stop a cab. When I met Miss Jones, I went to her room. She made some remarks about going out that night and robbing a cab. I argued against this and she asked for my gun and said she would go out herself."

Earlier in court under cross-examination, Jones had said: "He told me that he was a gunman back in Chicago and was operating a gang in London." Jones had also told the court that she was afraid of Hulten, who had reminded her several times that he had a loaded gun. She said he had even struck her once when she forgot to ask his permission to go downstairs to have a wash. Jones also declared that Hulten had kept all the money taken from Heath.

While on trial, and held in Holloway Prison, north London, Jones had written a dramatic letter to her co-accused saying: "If I get sent to prison it will kill my mother. So you see, Ricky, why you must tell the truth. Don't you think I've suffered enough?" Passages from the letter were read out in court, where both pleaded not guilty of murder. The letter also said: "You promised me in court you would tell the whole truth. Do not go back on your word Ricky." It continued: "What the police have against me is going through the man's pockets. Had you not ordered me to do so I would never have done it. But as my own life was in danger I did so. I could not believe you had done it, Ricky. I did not help you to carry him to the ditch. You know that. Ricky, for God's sake tell the truth. You and God are the only two who know of my innocence. Half of this case is fresh to me. The gun for instance – I did not know it was stolen. I did not know your real name, your age, your right rank. You were posing as an officer. I did not know you were married and had a child. I did not know you had deserted the Army. Why did you do it, Ricky, and why have you got me into this?"

Byrne, counsel for the Crown, was relentless in his cross-examination of Hulten. But, when the trial entered its last stage on 23rd January 1945, Maude made a dramatic appeal to the jury of nine men and three women on behalf of the American. He repeated several times: "Charity never faileth." He continued: "I beseech you, see that that little candle does not flicker out." He described Jones as being able to lie just as clearly as Hulten, but did not ask the jury to set his client free as he feared that the serviceman was responsible for manslaughter.

In his summing-up, Mr Justice Charles reiterated that Hulten had said he did not know that the trigger of the gun was back and the cartridge was in the breech. But he then asked the jury if they could believe a word of the story told by Hulten. Shaking his head, the judge said: "The cartridge could not get into the breech by accident. That needs a click." The judge went on to speak of the incredible cold-blooded brutality that followed the shooting and that Hulten neither knew, nor cared, whether the victim was alive or dead. The judge described how the victim had had his personal belongings removed from him while he lay dying on the passenger seat of his own car. "Accident? Was that an accident?" asked the judge, "Or was it murder?" Mr Justice Charles said that the jury were entitled to acquit the woman if they believed that she was forced into the matter against her will. Referring to the statement that Jones had wanted to be "thrilled", the judge said that she had found someone to give her a greater thrill than she had ever expected. He also spoke of the letter read to the court and surmised that Hulten had been intent on drawing the girl into "the net". Towards the close of his summing-up, the judge said: "Mr Maude has invited a verdict of manslaughter. I cannot exclude that from your consideration, but I am bound to tell you that the set of circumstances which Mr Maude puts forward as justifying a verdict of manslaughter do not concur with Hulten's description of what happened."

Hulten was convicted of the murder of George Heath and sentenced to death. At the end of January 1945, his family was thinking of appealing against the sentence to President Roosevelt or General Eisenhower. Elizabeth Jones had also been convicted of murder and sentenced to die. She was held in a heavily barred room at Holloway Prison. An appeal for both parties was held on 19th February 1945, where lawyers battled it out to save the convicted couple's lives. Both lost their appeals and the sentence of death was to stand. Hulten left the courtroom smiling slightly and joking with his guards as his fate was sealed. Jones was led away by two prison guards with no fuss.

The car in which Heath was killed was sold to car dealer George Page in Chippenham, who planned to auction the car. He had already had two bids for four-figure sums for the grey coupe, which remained in the hands of Scotland Yard. Both Hulten (held at Pentonville) and Jones (still in Holloway) were sentenced to die on 8th March 1945 but, at the end of February, 33,000 people were due to decide if they wished to save the young girl's life. The people of Neath, Glamorgan – Jones' hometown – received petition forms for her reprieve. Despite the fact that the residents of Neath strongly disapproved of the teenager's way of life, those backing the campaign were not convinced that she should die. It was reported in the press that even the mayor, Thomas Hughes, was considering a formal civic appeal to the home secretary. However, messages scrawled on walls in the town declared that Jones should hang.

Many of the town's residents declared that either both Hulten and Jones should hang or that both should be reprieved. Arthur Baker, 45, Jones' father, had tried in vain for people to sign the petition to save his daughter, but only 200 put pen to paper – mostly married women with daughters of their own – although many had also declared that Hulten should also be saved. In Glasgow, five young women working in a factory walked into the Sheriff's Court on 7th March protesting against a recommendation by the home secretary that Jones should be reprieved.

Hulten spent his last few hours quietly after attending mass at Wormwood Scrubs. He played chess with his guards before a van drew into the prison yard to take him to Pentonville. He exercised in the afternoon and wrote a farewell letter to his wife. He was not informed that Jones had, in fact, been given a reprieve. As he faced the scaffold on the morning of 8th March, there were scuffles outside Pentonville as a white lorry came hurtling towards the prison gates. A quick-thinking police inspector signalled to a lorry coming up the road to bar the entrance to the prison and a collision was avoided when the offending lorry swerved. It had been a small protest against capital punishment by the known campaigner Mrs Van der Elst, who was later charged at Clerkenwell Police Court of causing grievous bodily harm to Sergeant Horace Jarvis.

While Hulten hanged for his part in the murder, Jones was given a life sentence and her property was placed by magistrates in Neath in the care of her mother. A solicitor confirmed that eventually Jones would be released back into society, whereupon she would inherit the estate of Stanley Jones, her husband who was confirmed dead at Arnhem without having made a will. Hulten's and Jones' friendship had lasted only six days after they met on 3rd October 1944. During this time they knocked over and killed a nurse cycling along a country lane, as well as robbing a hitchhiker whom they knocked unconscious and threw into a river to drown. George Heath had been their final victim in just a few short days of "excitement" for Jones and death and destruction for Hulten. Jones was released from prison in May 1954 but her movements and whereabouts after she regained her freedom are still unknown today.

Notting Hill Riots

(1958)

Police reinforcements were rushed to Notting Hill Gate on the night of 31st August 1958 as race riots flared for the second time in 24 hours. Each time the riots began, gangs of white youths had jeered at their black counterparts and, each time, the incidents developed into violent clashes between opposing sides in Bramley Road. Eleven police cars raced to the area, where 400 people were yelling and brawling while hundreds more stood watching. As 50 officers tried to break up the fighting, they were jeered at by both sides. During the battle, builder Bert Harper of nearby Latimer Road was knifed in the neck by a black youth, who ran away as the man lay screaming on the pavement. An elderly woman was knocked flying by the mob and a boy of 10 was hit in the mouth with a broken bottle. A senior police officer said that by midnight 13 people had been arrested – nine of them were white. As the fights broke out, Labour MP for Kensington North, George Rogers, rang Scotland Yard asking them to send reinforcements. Rogers had received a call at his home in Harrow about the fights and was due to visit the Home Office on 2nd September to discuss the crisis. The fighting continued unabated for four hours while firemen fought a blaze caused by a home-made bomb, which was hurled through the basement window of the home of a 27-year-old Jamaican man. Police believed that the riots were initiated by small gangs of white youths intent on inflicting racial prejudice.

More rioting broke out on 1st September over a wide area of west London, and police reinforcements were once again called to Notting Hill as gangs of black and white youths clashed. More than 100 police officers were patrolling the trouble spots on what was the third night of violence, but as one incident was dealt with another one flared up. Thousands of people were milling round the streets and a police spokesman said the atmosphere was "electric". More than 36 people were arrested and many were found to be in possession of offensive weapons. Police threw a cordon around Notting Hill police station as a succession of Black Marias drew up outside with those arrested. In the battles that led to the night's arrests, rival gangs wielded bottles and iron bars. Gangs from other parts of London joined local youths thronging the area and some arrived in cars from which they jumped to join the mobs on the move. As the youths roved the streets, police reports came in of clashes in every part of Notting Hill.

In Bard Road, about 50 youths gathered outside a house and threw iron bars through the windows. The black people inside the house yelled at the mob and one white youth outside picked up a paraffin lamp and hurled it alight through a ground-floor window. The lamp landed on a bed that burst into flames and, as people inside the house fought the fire, a woman from inside dashed out into the street brandishing an axe. Earlier, hundreds of teenage youths – both boys and girls – marched through Oxford Gardens (close to Bramley Road) chanting that blacks were not welcome in the area, and a meat cleaver was hurled across the heads of the crowds, narrowly missing a black man.

Fights were also reported in Shepherd's Bush and Paddington, and a black man in the company of a white girl was attacked savagely by a gang of youths. He was taken to hospital with his face slashed, while his injured girlfriend was also treated. A bottle-battle broke out on the Paddington Harlesden boundaries when a gang of black youths was charged by a white gang; dozens of bottles were hurled by both sides. Another brawl started when two women from opposing sides began fighting and many of their peers joined in.

George Rogers requested that black policemen were drafted in to help stamp out the riots in his constituency. He demanded that plain-clothes officers could help on the ground. Meanwhile, the brawling continued, although youths gathered outside a restaurant in Harrow Road broke up when they saw police reinforcements in the area. The crowds on the third night of violence were somewhat bigger than the two nights previously. However, police confirmed that the actual brawling carried out was less. One young man, 26-year-old Seymour Manning from Jamaica, was attacked as he tried to flee a gang of youths. A cycle was thrown at him and cut his leg as he ran for cover in a nearby shop shouting: "Help me … they're going to kill me."

As those arrested were brought to court, the judge described the rioting as "disgraceful". Fourteen white men and one white woman, along with four black men, were charged with incidents arising out of the Bramley Road area, including insulting behaviour, possessing offensive weapons and assaulting police officers. Seventeen of those in court were remanded while two were fined. Meanwhile, in Nottingham, rioting broke out in the city and five men were jailed for their parts in various incidents. The newspapers reported that: "Every decent person in this country is ashamed of the outbreak of race rioting and hooliganism on British streets." Scotland Yard was looking into complaints that a "protection" racket was being imposed on black people living in the Notting Hill area.

Several people who ran clubs and cafes in west London told the police that they were being approached by members of a gang and promised "protection" for their premises for a fixed weekly payment. One club owner said that after he refused to pay for "protection" he was warned that he and his club would be put on the "riot" list, meaning that he could expect disturbances and damage. The police took these complaints extremely seriously and began an investigation into whether or not any organization was behind the riot clashes. The British public were outraged that this kind of organized crime could happen on its streets; there were calls in the press for the white hooligans found guilty of inciting race riots in London and Nottingham to be "dealt with by the courts with the utmost severity of the law. The guilty must suffer the maximum sentence."

One magistrate made an appeal for a voluntary curfew in Notting Hill Gate after he'd seen 28 people brought before him on charges. The magistrate, Mr Guest, said: "I deplore this violence. I had hoped that by now some civic, spiritual, or industrial or political leader of great influence in this neighbourhood would have had an opportunity to say something to assist the restoration of decent life there. As they had not taken the opportunity it might be useful if I said that now is the time for people of goodwill in that area to stay indoors from the early evening for a day or two at any rate ..."

The riots were attracting media comment from across the globe. The *Washington Post* said: "It is not for Americans to tell the British how to solve their race problems. This country has enough to do itself. Let us hope, however, that the British can avoid the costly mistakes the United States has made over the last 100 years in refusing so often to face up to the realities of segregation and its inherent inequalities." Moscow radio reported that "rampaging thugs" were attacking black people, while the *New York Times* stated: "There is something especially shocking about the race riots in England, and one may be sure that the British are themselves more shocked ... than anyone in foreign lands." The paper went on to state that: "The reasons for these attacks is economics and sex ... plus a measure of juvenile delinquency."

In early September 1958, Britain's trade union leaders were determined to take urgent action to help stop the rioting. The news was announced to an anxious Trades Union Congress in Bournemouth by the directing body – the General Council – which was likely to include the condemnation of outbreaks of hooliganism while urging union branches throughout the country to get to work to improve race relations between people. Some delegates were not satisfied that the steps would go far enough to be really effective. But, all were concerned that something should be done to "fight" the menace of racially motivated violence. One suggestion discussed was that the unions should be asked to take disciplinary measure against any member found guilty of taking part in, or inciting, race violence.

In a court case on 16th September 1958, Sir Gerald Dodson, the recorder at the Old Bailey, asked Sergeant Douglas Shearn how long the "trouble" had been brewing in the Notting Hill area and what was the major cause behind it. The police officer answered that there had been bad feeling between youths in the area for about 12 months owing to housing problems and mixed-race relationships. But, on the following day, a barrister, John Halnes, representing two out of 13 men accused of fighting and causing an affray, argued that the police had become "rattled" during the events of August and early September and had systematically gone about: "knocking everybody off". Halnes suggested that the young men arrested on the nights in question were "two a penny" as far as the police were concerned. Eight men – three of them black – were acquitted by the jury in the trial, but five others (all white) were jailed by the judge for periods ranging from 18 months to two years.

Passing sentence, Judge Sir Gerald Dodson told them: "You have been convicted of what amounts to brawling in the streets, which was common enough in England many years ago when ignorance and violence were rampant. Out of the chaos of those times, a law against affrays emerged in order to deal with the rowdiness of that time. As society progressed and learned better manners, that precise law became unnecessary. But by your conduct you have put the clock back nearly 300 years and disgraced yourselves and your families." The judge was backed by Dr Geoffrey Fisher, the then Archbishop of Canterbury, who told bishops attending the Convocation of Canterbury at Lambeth Palace in London that it was shocking in Britain that there should be "such exhibitions of racial animosity and hatred". The church recommended that greater attention should be given to ethnic minorities in Britain.

When the riots broke out, it had just been 14 years since the end of the Second World War and Britain had seen an influx of migrants whom the country's working-class youths despised. Their open hostility was exploited and inflamed by Far Right groups with "Keep Britain White" slogans, such as the White Defence League and the Union Movement. This undoubtedly led to horrific scenes of violence, incited and controlled by organized groups intent on persecuting innocent youths and their families.

Gunther Podola

(1959)

On 14th July 1959, a beautiful 32-year-old model who talked to a gunman just minutes before he murdered 43-year-old Detective Sergeant Raymond Purdy was being guarded by police in fear of her life. Joan Schiffman, who was married to an American, had become familiar to millions of viewers in 1956 when she worked as a hostess on the ITV programme *Double Your Money*, but she had put her life in danger by inadvertently becoming involved with the gunman who burgled her flat in Rowland Gardens, London. Furs, jewellery, documents and two passports were stolen and, three weeks later, Mrs Schiffman received a telephone call from a man demanding money for the return of the passports. Two more phone calls were made to the robbed woman, who had been in touch with police over the incidents. The police tried to trace the calls, but each time the man rang off before engineers could pinpoint his location.

The fourth telephone call came on Monday, 14th July. Engineers finally managed to trace the call and, while the man was being kept on the phone, Detective Sergeant Purdy and his colleague Detective Sergeant John Sandford approached him in a telephone kiosk. The man ran from the scene but was chased by the detectives, who eventually arrested him in the entrance to a block of flats in Onslow Square. While Sandford went to call for a police car, Purdy was shot through the heart by the man who then proceeded to flee the scene. It was for this reason that Joan Schiffman – who did not know the man who had been telephoning her – was under armed guard. She knew the man's voice and it was feared that the killer, knowing that if caught he would hang for shooting a police officer, might try to claim a second victim. Scotland Yard named Gunther Podola as a man they believed could help with their inquiries. The Yard then received a tip-off from someone who knew that German-born Podola was known to be friendly with a blonde woman – Sally – who was often seen close to Wardour Street in London's West End. The hunt was then on to find the woman, while further calls to the Yard confirmed that Podola frequented clubs in the Soho area. Pictures of Podola were sent to Scotland Yard on 16th July from Canada, the country from which the 30-year-old German was deported in 1958, and the country of his birth.

On 17th July, a man in shirtsleeves lay on a small divan bed in a London hotel reading a magazine. He was listening to pop music when the door suddenly burst open and in came five detectives. The three-day search for Gunther Fritz Podola had come to an end in room 15 of Claremont House Hotel in Queen's Gate, South Kensington, just 300 paces away from Onslow Square where Detective Sergeant Purdy, a married father of three, was shot dead. The police were led by Detective Superintendent David Hislop, who stayed in room 15 for a full 30 minutes before coming down from the third floor with the suspect. Podola had been arrested.

The following day, the police issued a statement: "Podola is in

Metropolitan Police custody and is at present in a general ward of a London hospital to which he was admitted on the advice of a doctor who saw him after his arrest. We are authorized by the hospital to say that he is not seriously ill and has undergone no operation. We further point out that the circumstances of his arrest cannot be disclosed, as this information will be given in evidence in court after he has been charged." It was known that Podola was suffering from mental and physical exhaustion. Meanwhile, police found a suitcase containing clothing, several passports, a gun and ammunition in the attic of the London hotel.

The services of a solicitor were secured for Podola due to the suspect being an alien who was probably friendless and penniless. But, for almost a week after his arrest, the German remained unfit for interview. However, on 20th July he appeared in court, with a black eye and bruise to his top lip, charged with the murder of Detective Sergeant Purdy. In the House of Commons, the home secretary strenuously denied that the suspect had been beaten up in the police station. It took just four minutes in court to remand the accused. Podola was represented by Frederick Williams, who asked the court for legal aid before the prisoner was taken to Brixton Prison. He left court supported by the two detectives who had held him up during the four-minute hearing before being driven to the hospital wing of the prison. MPs were worried about the condition of Podola and the fact that he had been taken to hospital just a few hours after his arrest.

On 23rd July, in response to an inquiry requested by Lord

Stonham, Lord Chancellor Viscount Kilmuir ruled that no further discussions could be allowed at that time about the injuries suffered by Podola. The prisoner on remand made his second court appearance on 28th July, where he was still seen to have a black eye. Hislop asked for a further remand, but the magistrate, Guest, would only remand until 4th August when he hoped the case would be opened. Williams then told the magistrate that this caused him some difficulty because, due to medical reasons, he was not able to obtain adequate instructions for the defence. Podola was once again remanded before being taken back to the hospital wing of the prison. On 4th August, at Podola's third court appearance, Williams once again stated that he'd had difficulty in obtaining instructions for the defence. Guest agreed to remand the case for a further 10 days.

At the time, the case was expected to make legal history as the first murder case in England in which no evidence about the killing was reported in the press. On 11th August, there were two indications that this might happen. First, the magistrate agreed that the details of the murder should be heard in closed court. Second, it was believed that Podola could have lost his memory and that a jury might find him not fit to plead. It was rumoured that the public might never know the events surrounding how Detective Sergeant Purdy lost his life. At the time, legal experts were in agreement that this was the first time that a murder case involved all the lower court hearings being held in secret.

The accused was then sent for a further hearing at the Old Bailey on 14th August, where Joan Schiffman gave evidence in secret. For five hours behind locked doors at London's Tower Bridge court, Podola listened while 18 witnesses told their stories. The press and public had been allowed into the court for precisely two minutes and 28 seconds. After Podola was led into court and took his place in the dock, the court was cleared.

The trial began on 10th September when the accused made a two-minute appearance in Court 1. The jury of 10 men and two women were asked to decide whether or not Podola had lost his memory of events before his arrest, and were asked to say if the loss of memory amounted to insanity, which would make him unfit to plead "guilty" or "not guilty" to the charge of murder. But, Maxwell Turner, the senior treasury counsel leading the prosecution, opposed the loss of memory submission. Meanwhile, it came to light that Podola was amazed and surprised to learn that he had shot someone, and his solicitor, Williams, confirmed that he had still not received any instructions. Podola was asked in court to recall events in his life prior to when police descended on his hotel room but still claimed that he remembered nothing of his life before his arrest in July. But, in fact, Podola had received a postcard in prison from a man claiming to be a friend, Starkey. He referred to Podola as Mike (he had assumed the alias Mike Colato after his arrival in London in May 1959) and the prisoner duly wrote back to the man saying he'd been pleasantly surprised to hear from him. When Starkey appeared in court, Podola claimed not to know him. Turner, acting for the prosecution, questioned the prisoner's response to the postcard in which he seemed to know Starkey and had asked him how he was keeping. The end of the postcard read: "I don't want to bore you. I've got into this thing, and I'll have to see it through, no matter what."

Turner asked: "What did you mean by that?" Podola replied: "Well, if he knows I am in prison, he will probably know why I am in."

Several doctors gave evidence in the case as to whether or not Podola had indeed lost his memory. His eye injury was described as having happened when the door to his hotel room was opened by police; it was then claimed that Podola had been placed on the bed and given first-aid treatment. Some doctors claimed that the accused's loss of memory was genuine. Dr Edward Larkin told the court that Podola would have had to be extremely consistent, and that pretending in the way the prosecution claimed was impossible due to the fact that it would take too much intelligence to keep up the pretence – and a huge knowledge of psychiatric matters. But, Turner claimed: "Here is a man with the strongest motive in the world, simulating amnesia. A man who, in fact, may well have been slightly concussed which, together with his physical exhaustion, possible lack of food etc. could explain his physical condition after his arrest. A man who then, in order to avoid the consequences of his crime, pretends to have lost his memory."

Lawton, QC, acting for Podola, then cross-examined Detective Inspector Peter Vibart – part of the arresting party from Scotland Yard – and accused the senior officer of lying under oath about the exact words used when the prisoner was told in hospital that he was to be charged with murder. The policeman's notebook was then examined by the judge and jury to see whether or not they thought it had been tampered with. The officer denied the allegation by the defence. Dr Denis Leigh, who examined the prisoner for the Crown, was convinced that Podola was lying about his loss of memory.

Turner gave his summing-up speech for the prosecution to the court on 21st September and suggested that Podola made "two terrible mistakes". He was referring to medical evidence about the amount of psychiatric knowledge which it was said Podola would have needed in order to give the answers he had – and that the two mistakes were unlikely if the loss of memory were genuine. The first mistake was the prisoner's claim that his loss of memory affected events covering the whole of his life. This was extremely rare because people only usually lost memory of a terrible fear; the brain then protected the person from that fear by blocking it. It was unlikely that Podola had lost his entire memory from his young years. The second mistake was that he had not exhibited other symptoms associated with memory loss. The jury decided that the defendant was pretending to have lost his memory and found him fit for trial. During a formal charge of murdering Detective Sergeant Raymond Purdy, the German answered: "Not guilty".

Podola was found guilty of murder on 24th September 1959, when a black-capped judge sentenced him to death. He had failed to convince the second jury that he had lost his memory. It had taken 10 men and two women just 38 minutes to find him guilty. As the judge spoke, Podola gripped the edge of the dock with both hands, while staring down into the courtroom. He was led away to the cells following the sentencing – and the case that made legal history in England came to an end. The prisoner was taken to the death cell at Wandsworth Prison while the events of his life – which he claimed not to remember – came to light.

He had turned from being a cheap little crook into a professional housebreaker and finally the killer of a London policeman. He hadn't had much of a start in life and, at age 10, had watched as his father left to join the Nazis in the Second World War. His father was killed on the Russian front and Podola was left to look after his mother. He enrolled in the Hitler Youth Movement at age 13 and became an apprentice aircraft designer with Focke-Wulf. At 15, he gained his first and only certificate of merit – as a qualified glider pilot. But Podola's world of achievement was short-lived when Adolf Hitler was found dead. Podola survived the post-war fallout in Berlin through living a life of cunning, lying and stealing. In 1952, there was little future in East Berlin for Podola and he escaped to West Berlin before emigrating to Canada.

On a farm near Montreal, he worked as a labourer before finding out that his sweetheart in Berlin had married an American soldier. It was the catalyst that changed Podola's life to one of crime: he dreamed of being a gangster and influential gunman. He began to hate the law and all it stood for and began life as a burglar. His crimes in Montreal and around Canada led to two years' imprisonment before he was eventually deported back to Germany. After failing to make anything of his life in Germany, Podola left his native homeland with a forged West German passport in his pocket and the names and contact details of dozens of Soho underworld criminals. Podola wanted fame and notoriety in London on the side of the law that he knew best. He wanted to be revered by other gangsters – he was convinced he was one – and he wanted to be feared and admired in equal measure.

He did not appeal his conviction and was due to be executed on 16th October 1959, but the German Embassy in London wanted to appeal on his behalf – there was no death penalty in Germany. His execution date was then cancelled and his case set for the appeal courts. However, the five appeal judges decided that the sentence would stand for the death of Purdy. A new bid to save him was then made, whereby his case should be considered by the House of Lords. The appeal was refused and the date of his execution was given as 5th November. The man who had lived the last few months of his life on the fringe of London's underworld was visited by a priest in order to prepare for his own death.

A crowd of nearly 100 people gathered outside Wandsworth Prison as Podola was executed. He entered the history books as the last man to be hanged in Britain for killing a police officer. Reports in some of the following day's newspapers – that the condemned had made a will leaving his worldly possessions to a fund in aid of Detective Sergeant Raymond Purdy's widow – were declared untrue.

The Shepherd's Bush Murders

(1966)

The underworld was beginning to squeal in August 1966 when the cold-blooded slayers of three London detectives broke down the code of silence among even the hardest criminals. Several names and addresses had been passed to the police and the three killers were believed to be well known in the world of crime, and to have many criminal contacts. Sir Joseph Simpson, the Metropolitan Police commissioner, told the BBC on 14th August: "I have no doubt we will get to the bottom of this." Sir Joseph also promised full police protection for anyone coming forward with information and informed the general public that they had nothing to fear. Later that night, a man who told the police that he had sold the car used by the killers only an hour before the killings was held at Shepherd's Bush police station – the home of the murder hunt's headquarters. The man had spent two days in the station while teams of Flying Squad detectives swooped on houses near the scene of the massacre in Braybrook Street.

Meanwhile, Chief Superintendent Richard Lewis, who was in charge of Britain's prisons, paid a visit to Wormwood Scrubs – which overlooked the murder scene. The prison held 900 prisoners, many of whom were considered escape risks, and Lewis needed to establish if there had been any unrest at the prison on the day of the murders as detectives believed that the killers might have been planning to organize an escape from the jail. Following the deaths of the three detectives, one prisoner (serving a five-year sentence) was moved to another London prison.

At least one of the dead detectives was thought to have known the killers. A senior detective said: "The detective in question was well known for being cautious, and also for having a great deal of information about underworld characters. We think he must have had a good reason for closing in at that time." The first big break in the hunt came with the discovery of the killers' car, which was one of several vehicles in a Lambeth lock-up garage found on 14th August. Police were still appealing for anyone who saw the car in the hours before the killings to come forward.

As squads of detectives replaced men going off duty, they were reissued with firearms and told to shoot if necessary. The families of the dead detectives – Detective Sergeant Christopher Head, 30, Detective Constable David Wombwell, 25, and Constable Geoffrey Fox, 25, – received cash donations that had poured into police stations all over Britain ever since the murders had occurred. Meanwhile, the killers' car was found after a tip-off. The blue Vanguard – registration number PGT 726 – was discovered in Tinworth Street when squad cars dashed to the scene and smashed a padlock on a garage beneath a gloomy railway arch. The area was immediately cordoned off and fingerprint experts worked the scene until the car was driven away by police. The detectives in the hunt were approached by a housewife who had seen the car being put in the garage on the day of the murders. "I was with a friend," she said. "We saw this old blue car being driven up the yard way to the end garage. We noticed it particularly because it was going fast."

Then, on 15th August, 36-year-old John (Jack) Witney, from Paddington, was arrested in connection with the murders. He appeared at West London Magistrates Court the following day, while the hunt continued for the two other men whom police believed could help with their inquiries. They were confident that arrests would be made within a day or two. That same day, the press printed a number of statements from some of the country's most influential men. Lord Chief Justice Parker said: "There is no room for sympathy for criminals who are out to make war on society. It is war, and war in cold blood." The secretary of the Police Federation said: "London and other large cities are in danger of being dominated by gangs of organized criminals. They are desperate men who will stop at nothing. Urgent action must be taken to strengthen the police and reform the law to secure convictions." The final quote of the day came from a former attorney general, Lord Shawcross, who said: "One reason why crime in Britain is booming is that more and more people are getting away with it. We persist in treating the detection and trial of criminals as a kind of game to be played according to some sort of Queensbury rules. But it isn't a game. It is a war, which we are losing because we won't fight it. In seeking to ensure that no innocent man is convicted, we fall over backwards in protecting the guilty."

The home secretary, Roy Jenkins, told the public that

underworld criminals threatened the whole fabric of society. He said: "Today we have a real menace to society, both in organized criminal conspiracies and individual acts of violence. Unless we can control the mounting crime wave, we shall get a climate hostile to individual liberty. Therefore, the battle against crime must have first priority. The present position is terrifying a lot of people, involving vast economic losses. I recognize the urgent need for some new laws. In the autumn I propose to present to parliament by far the biggest and most wide-ranging measure in this sphere since 1948." Jenkins wanted to take a real stance in halting crime, especially with regard to bringing the "big fish" to trial. He stated that these were the criminals who were getting away with "murder" and had shown themselves able to frustrate the processes of justice.

Violence was becoming an inherent element of professional crime. Violence and corruption were being used to intimidate witnesses, particularly those involved in identifying criminals, and to intimidate jurors and police officers. The police were convinced that behind violent crime lay a terrible world of misery and fear and unbelievable callousness. One senior court official stated that cleaning-up known criminal gangs in special operations should be made a priority. It was well known that particularly dangerous criminals faced trial but ended up being acquitted because of loopholes in the legal system and intimidation. The message from the men at the top was simple: if beating professional crime was not made a priority, then Britain would never win the war against its underworld gangsters.

By 17th August 1966, Scotland Yard was hunting John Duddy, 37, and Harry Roberts, 30, in connection with the deaths of the three police detectives five days earlier. The police appealed for public information that would lead to the arrest of the men, but they warned the public not to approach them; they were armed and dangerous. Squad cars carrying armed officers sped away from Shepherd's Bush, but no details were given from the patrol-car radios in case the conversations were overheard. Police were hunting for the men in Southall, Bristol and London. It was believed that Roberts used the alias Ronald Hall or John O'Brien, while Glaswegian Duddy was known to have scars and tattoos. Meanwhile, their alleged accomplice John Witney was watched by a crowd of 300 spectators as he entered court, which was attended by his wife Lily. The 15-minute hearing resulted in the man being remanded. His head was bowed as the charges were read.

In September, the home secretary travelled to the US to see if he could pick up "some new ammunition" in Britain's fight against crime. He saw Senator John McClellan, who was in command of the Senate Crime Investigation Committee and knew how to flush top crooks out of their hideouts, how to identify the "big fish" and how to put them where the public could see them and the police could get to them. McClellan had 100 major prosecutions to his name and it was hoped that the gang-busting senator could help Roy Jenkins. McClellan stated that Britain was facing the start of a crime network in which importance should be placed on identifying the men behind it in public. He claimed that public anger and support was the best weapon.

McClellan suggested that Britain should set up an investigating committee under the Tribunals of Inquiry Act, with the specific task of pinning down the men behind the country's gangs. Jenkins was due to be given the latest draft of the new Criminal Justice Bill on 3rd October. The first changes to be brought in were majority verdicts, which meant that if 10 jurors agreed then the decision to convict was carried – so that if two members of the jury had been bribed or intimidated, then the right outcome would prevail. The second change involved excluding convicted criminals from sitting in judgement on the jury. There was also a suggestion that everyone's fingerprints should be kept on file. The measures – should they be introduced – were intended to strike fear into the heart of the criminal underworld. It was also planned that the rules restricting detective work and trying to take statements should be changed and that more modern crime-fighting equipment – from helicopters to CCTV and computers – should be used. The US committee was able to call anyone it wished for questioning under oath and if a witness failed to turn up then they faced jail for contempt. Jail was also on offer for those committing perjury. "Big fish" gangster Frank Costello had been pinned down in this way. He had sweated all day under pressure from questioning and eventually admitted that he had $45,000 in a safe-deposit box. He was eventually jailed for contempt and tax evasion. Hearings had also exposed vast gambling rackets, bribery and corruption in official offices and Murder, Inc. was revealed as a monstrous company of men renting themselves out as assassins. The result of the hearings gave the US a significant lull in organized crime; many civic officials were "retired" or sacked. The gangsters involved, although not thwarted entirely, were either jailed or slithered back into their holes, marked for life. The most spectacular of McClellan's hearings dealt with the Mafia's "Cosa Nostra" gang: assassin Joe Vaiachi went from jail to the hearings and disclosed the names of his former fellow directors in an enormous crime industry. One by one, a tawdry bunch of men was barraged by questions from the committee and 80 million viewers tuned in to watch a daily catalogue of crime including dope, vice, murder and extortion. The public was able to watch absolutely everything that the committee was investigating, and it made a big difference.

Meanwhile, back in Britain, the hunt was still on for Roberts and a picture of him was released in the press with a warning to the public not to go near him, but to call their nearest police station. A major hunt for the Londoner began in Epping Forest, where he was believed to be in hiding in the High Beech area of Essex. Trippers and courting couples were ordered out of the area while police, armed with tear gas, hunted by floodlight between Theydon Bois and Robin Hood roundabout.

Duddy was picked up in a Glasgow tenement on 17th August. He put up no resistance to the arrest and was flown to London before being driven to Shepherd's Bush police station. The Glasgow swoop on a crumbling housing estate took place following earlier night raids on several other addresses in the city. By the time Duddy arrived at his destination in London, there was a crowd of 500 waiting outside the station.

In Epping Forest, hunters were stalking along with 500 police officers. The group had 6,000 acres to cover by foot in the search for Roberts, a former Army sniper in Malaya. It was a daunting task shadowed with possibilities of dread, as all searchers knew that the man they were seeking probably had three weapons, including a rifle. Roberts, who had once been a hunter in forests and jungles, had become the hunted. Police stumbled upon a fire where there were signs of a hurried retreat and a squirrel was found being cooked in an old saucepan.

Roberts' wife, Margaret, appealed to her husband to give himself up. She was under police protection from the man whom she had left eight years previously, as Mrs Roberts was aware that her husband had been trying to find her some two months before the murders. Yet Roberts had simply vanished and police could find no further trace of him, although Interpol had circulated his picture to 95 countries. Meanwhile, a grim two-day hunt of Epping Forest had drawn a blank.

Angry crowds hissed and booed Duddy as he was taken into court in London on 19th August 1966. He was remanded in custody charged with the murders of the three policemen. Then, detectives received vital clues in their hunt for Roberts when a woman – whose identity was kept secret – came forward. For four hours, the woman sat talking to senior detectives in a locked room at Shepherd's Bush police station. The woman was regarded as a vital witness and was taken home after the meeting, where she was put under constant guard. Another woman, June Howard, had also come forward as Roberts' landlady from Maida Vale, where he lodged both before and after the shooting. By the time the police put out a public appeal, Roberts had left her home. By 23rd August, having compiled a file on the hunted man's life, police were convinced that there were only three people who would harbour Roberts; all three were missing from their usual haunts.

On 24th August, it was revealed that the three murdered detectives were to be paid the nation's highest tribute with a memorial service at Westminster Abbey. The service – held on 6th September – would make history: the memory of police officers who fell in the line of duty had not been honoured in this way for more than half a century. It was hoped that the Queen and Prime Minister Harold Wilson would lead the mourners.

Nearing the end of August, police believed that they had virtually closed in on Roberts when a Scotland Yard detective tailed a man in King's Cross, but the man escaped after a chase through the streets. Within minutes 300 police officers were combing the area searching empty schools, warehouses, factories and railway yards, but no sign of the wanted man was found.

On 25th August, Roberts' mother made a dramatic appeal to her son to give himself up. With her face masked by shadows, the distraught woman pleaded: "I ask you from the bottom of my heart to come into the open and give yourself up. If you make an appointment with me, I will come with you. The whole thing is killing

me. Please do as I ask you, before there is any more bloodshed."
The appeal was screened on both BBC and ITV news bulletins. Her son had been on the run for 13 days and, on the 14th day, a poorly dressed "rough" squad were sent out on to the streets to search the Camden Town area of London, while a smartly dressed "smooth" squad moved among clubs in Mayfair and other parts of central London. Roberts could move in both circles easily.

On Thursday 1st September, Chris Head, David Wombwell and Geoffrey Fox were given a funeral in London. The police and the victims' families did not mourn alone: 5,000 people stood silently in the rain to pay their tribute as the funeral procession moved through west London. They saw the coffins of the three policemen carried into the Church of St Stephen with St Thomas, just opposite Shepherd's Bush station. Duddy, meanwhile, told detectives that it was Roberts who had started the shooting. He added: "I just grabbed a gun and ran to the police car and shot the driver through the window. I must have been mad. I wish you could hang me now."

At West London Magistrates Court on 14th September, Oliver Nugent, prosecuting, talked of the crime "which has horrified the whole nation". Nugent went on to describe how the police were making strenuous efforts to find the third man, Harry Roberts, as Duddy and Witney appeared for the first time in the dock together. Each was charged with murdering the three detectives. Opening for the prosecution, Nugent described how the three officers had been shot close to Wormwood Scrubs in Braybrook Street on Friday, 12th August. The scene immediately after the shooting was shown in photographs, which were given to the magistrate. Wombwell was shown lying on his back about 10 yards behind the police car. The engine had still been running and the back wheels were spinning. The obstruction stopping the car from moving forward was the body of Chris Head, who had been shot in the back. Fox was shown in the driver's seat, shot through the head. As Fox died, the car lurched forward and went over the body of Sergeant Head, who was not dead at the time but died soon after. Two weapons had been used, a 0.38 Service revolver and a Luger 9mm automatic. Neither weapon had been found.

On the day of the murders, Witney had been interviewed about his "scruffy" car, but claimed that he'd sold it for £15 to a man he didn't know. Witney stuck to his story for quite a long time, but when the car was found by police in a garage rented by the accused, it was clear he had been involved. Overalls and part of a stocking had been found in the car along with three 0.38 cartridges. The overalls and stocking were probably the reason why the Vanguard Estate had been stopped by the three officers. Fingerprint evidence also showed that all three men – the two accused and the missing man – had been in the car and that all three were known to associate on a regular basis. All three had been living at an address in Wymering Road, Paddington, at some point.

On 10th October, a massive dragnet on criminals' hideouts started in Dublin after an underworld tip-off that Roberts had gone into hiding there. Detectives swooped on drinking clubs, dockland bars and cafes in the hunt for the 30-year-old Roberts. The tip-off was so strong that two Scotland Yard detectives flew to the emerald isle, where Irish police made it clear they would co-operate fully with the Yard men. On 14th October, a tent in a woodland hideout believed to have been used by Roberts was found by a farmer near Bishop's Stortford in Hertfordshire. The occupant had left his dwelling, and his camping gear, in a hurry. The man leading the hunt for the fugitive, Superintendent Richard Chitty, had just returned from Ireland when the vital clue to Roberts' whereabouts was discovered. Chitty had been attending the opening days of the trial of both Duddy and Witney at the Old Bailey when he heard the news. Meanwhile, three schoolchildren, a 14-year-old girl and two 10-year-old boys, played with a jigsaw puzzle at the Old Bailey as they waited to give their witness statements about the murders. One of the boys said he thought he'd been watching a film when he witnessed the shootings in Shepherd's Bush, until he realized that there were no cameras and that the action was for real. Both Duddy and Witney pleaded not guilty to murder.

On 15th November, a hooded man was led into Shepherd's Bush police station. The man was Harry Roberts, covered in a blanket and caught, at last. He was charged with the murders of the three detectives and appeared at West London Magistrates Court on the following day. He had been arrested in a farmer's fodder store near Bishop's Stortford and the news halted the trial at the Old Bailey of his co-accused. The trial was suspended while further legal stages in the case were agreed. Roberts' 95 days on the run had ended dramatically, without violence.

He was discovered by 33-year-old Sergeant Peter Smith who was part of a party ordered to ring the wooded area. Smith had spotted a disused hangar and, armed with a revolver, had walked into the building alone. The hangar was filled with bales of straw and Smith noticed a bottle of methylated spirits and evidence that someone had been sleeping there. The police officer, who had been switched from his usual M1 traffic patrol, then found a sleeping bag, complete with a body inside. He prodded the man and Roberts poked his head out. Roberts – who looked tired and withdrawn – gave Smith no resistance and quietly gave himself up to the police officer and his colleague, 44-year-old Sergeant John Thorne. The discovery had come about when 21-year-old traveller John Cunningham was out hunting in Thorley Wood and came across a tent set in the undergrowth. The information he gave to the police was to spark the final hunt for Roberts when fingerprints found on a gun holster in the tent launched a full-scale search of the area. On 16th November, detectives dug up a mud-covered revolver in a dramatic dawn search on which they took Roberts. Carried out on Hampstead Heath, the search followed the prisoner's first night in custody. Roberts indicated a spot past the famous beauty spot's fairground site, several yards from a public footpath under trees. After then appearing briefly at the magistrates court, he was taken for an even briefer appearance at the Old Bailey, where legal steps were taken to arrange for him to be tried jointly with Duddy and Witney.

In December 1966, Lilian Perry told the Old Bailey how she

had first lied to the police about Roberts, because he was on the run and she was "terrified" that he would shoot her, too. She later told the truth to a magistrates court – that she had seen Roberts following the murders – but was still frightened. Perry had travelled on a bus to Epping Forest with Roberts who told her: "This is as far as we go together. I am on my own now." The court then heard on 8th December how Witney was also terrified of Roberts. He claimed that Roberts had killed two of the officers and that Duddy had killed the other. Witney claimed that Roberts was a different person after shooting the two men in cold blood. Roberts allegedly asked Witney if he would grass on him and said: "Don't make that mistake. You know what happened to Jack Spot and his wife – and that was minor by comparison." (In 1956, Jack "Spot" Comer, a known gangster and his wife Rita were attacked in the street by "Mad Frankie" Fraser, Bobby Warren and around six others on the orders of rival gangster Billy Hill. Fraser repeatedly stabbed Spot using a butcher's chopper and didn't expect to be repaid for the attack as he hoped that such a high-profile knifing would earn him an unparalleled reputation on London's streets.)

All three men were convicted for the murders in a crime that was described as the most heinous [crime] committed in this country for a generation or more. Following the Murder (Abolition of Death Penalty) Act 1965, each faced at least 30 years in prison, a minimum term recommended by the judge, Justice Glyn-Jones, after he gave them life sentences at the Old Bailey on 12th December 1966. Each was also given 10 years – to run concurrently – for illegally possessing firearms. It was also learned that the police involved in the country's biggest manhunt had hardly slept while they carried out what they called "Operation Shepherd".

Roberts was taken under heavy guard to Parkhurst Prison on the Isle of Wight, where many of the country's closely guarded criminals were held. Duddy was switched to the security wing at Leicester Prison, where he was to join three of the Great Train Robbers; and Witney was transported to Wakefield, where he was to join around 100 murderers also serving life sentences. Roberts was then believed to have been moved to Wandsworth Prison in April 1967 when he was due to give evidence at Inner London Sessions in connection with a charge against a man who was alleged to have sold him three revolvers. Christos Costas, 30, was convicted of selling guns to scar-faced killer Roberts and was given six years. The court chairman told the sessions that: "This is a classic example of the dangers of having transactions with firearms in the criminal world."

In March 1973, a collection of implements brought Roberts within inches of escaping his top-security prison cell, when an almost complete jail-breaking kit – including a home-made drill, wire cutters and a compass – were found. On 21st March, a jury heard how all that was missing was a pair of heavy bolt cutters to get through two wire-mesh barriers. The items had been smuggled into Parkhurst Prison by Roberts' 73-year-old mother, but the cutters were intercepted by prison officers before they could reach him. Dorothy Roberts pleaded not guilty of trying to help her son escape. The bolt cutters were found in a washroom where Roberts would have been due to visit later that day in order to fetch a blackboard and easel (stored there) when he attended a French lesson with train robber Charles Wilson. It was then discovered that Roberts had a hole in the wall of his cell – hidden behind his bed – with escape equipment inside. Dorothy Roberts was cleared of the charge on 29th March 1973.

Duddy died in jail, at Parkhurst, on 8th February 1981. He was 52 years old and had suffered a number of heart attacks the previous year. By this time, the era of the supergrass had begun. In 1972, a robbery at a branch of Barclays Bank in Wembley, west London, saw suspect Bertie Smalls offering to turn Queen's evidence on every crime he knew about in return for immunity. The director of public prosecutions agreed and Smalls gave evidence that led to major convictions on 20 crimes. However, the fear with supergrasses was that they would crack when faced with their old "mates" in court. Smalls was one of them, but after one of his former gang members crudely called his wife "Slack Alice" the supergrass never faltered. The second supergrass known to the police was a bank robber called Maurice O'Mahoney who wanted to outdo Smalls and earn himself the title "King of the Squealers". He turned supergrass despite threats that his eyes would be gouged out. O'Mahoney's evidence resulted in 200 convictions, and he and Smalls made it plain that the criminal underworld would have to watch its collective "back" when supergrasses became a vital police weapon.

While Smalls may have been the first recognized criminal turned informer, there were many underworld characters who had been willing to give up Roberts to Scotland Yard. After serving 30 years for the murders, Roberts gave an interview to the *Daily Mirror* in which he stated that even though he could possibly be paroled later in 1996, he didn't wish to be. He said: "I killed cops in cold blood and I know society will never forgive me for that. One day, perhaps, it will be right for me to go free – but I know that time isn't now." Outraged MPs and police begged the then home secretary, Michael Howard, to reject the idea of Roberts being given parole. The news that Roberts might be given parole saw Constable Geoff Fox's son Paul give a heartfelt newspaper interview, in which he said that his father would have loved to have spent his days fishing. In the same interview, he slammed Roberts for dreaming of his freedom.

Witney had been freed on parole in 1991. In April 1999, aged 69, he was found battered to death in his Bristol home. His death was not thought to have had a connection to his earlier conviction. Just a year later, Roberts was moved to an open prison in Suffolk on recommendations of the parole board. It was the first step towards his release. However, the convicted killer blew his chances of freedom after it was discovered in 2001 that he had conned jail chiefs. He had been on day release to attend a job, but instead was found meeting up with old criminal friends in London. Information from a secret source was also passed from the home secretary, David Blunkett, to the parole board, who kept the killer inside. Roberts lost a high court bid to be allowed to see the information that robbed him of his freedom. The Appeal Court upheld the decision not to allow Roberts to see the information and stated that: "The source would be at real risk if the material was shown to Roberts." The convicted killer had tried to escape 22 times from prison. He renewed his bid for freedom in April 2005, but it seemed that the Home Office was trying to keep him in jail until he died, based on evidence that it refused to disclose; the sensitive information was believed to show that Roberts was still dangerous. The parole board decided in 2006 that he should not be set free or transferred to an open jail. He launched a fresh appeal in 2008. In 2009, the parole board still considered Roberts a threat to society and he remains in prison in Cambridgeshire.

Brass Handles Murders

(2006)

In a bizarre turn of events, two hit-men were killed as they tried to make their getaway from a pub on 12th March 2006. The two men were executed by other drinkers before they could reach their getaway car. Witnesses said that two Asian men, wearing leather gloves, ran into the pub and blasted the men drinking at the bar. As they fled, they were chased and caught about 75 yards away from the murder scene. In what appeared to be gangland-style executions, one man was blasted through the back of the head as he knelt down, while the other was shot in the back.

A witness who was too scared to give his name, said: "We were watching the Manchester United-Newcastle game when two men walked in. They had woolly beanie hats on but suddenly lowered them over their faces," revealing that they were really balaclavas. He continued: "They began shooting and shot two lads. They ran out and a group of people ran after them. The gunmen appeared to be rushing to a black Mondeo, but they got shot on wasteland before they could reach it. It was terrifying."

A number of children had also witnessed the horrific shooting and the father of one youngster claimed: "My son was playing football with his pals when the men dashed out of the pub. One was kneeling down and was shot through the back of the head.

The other was shot in the back. All the lads were stood around the man who had the back of his head shot off." Paramedics who arrived within minutes found the men already dead. They covered the bodies with white sheets.

It was believed that the shooting at the Brass Handles pub in Salford, Greater Manchester, was linked to a turf war between rival gangs from Manchester and Salford. Armed police shadowed by a force helicopter flooded the Pendleton area while the two men shot at the bar were rushed to Hope Hospital. Leor Giladi of Greater Manchester police said: "This horrific incident happened in a packed pub while fans watched football. Two mixed-raced men have died and two white men are receiving hospital treatment. Their condition is serious." He then added: "Gang warfare has been a problem in the past here, but we don't yet know the full motive. We have a large police presence here and we are urging calm among the local community and appeal for any witnesses to come forward."

The double murder came just three days after a 37-year-old man was blasted in the neck by two men. The motive for the shooting was unknown at the time and the victim remained in a stable condition in North Manchester General Hospital.

On the following day, four men in their early twenties were quizzed about the gangland pub shoot-out. Detectives believed that the two gunmen who burst into the pub wanted revenge for a near-fatal stabbing. One witness claimed that one of the white men shot in the pub was: "Giving people tenners minutes before it kicked off, saying 'Remember my name'." The two men who survived were David Totton and Aaron Travers, both 27, while the two dead men were named as Richard Austin, 19, and Carlton Alveranga, 20. The police were met with a wall of silence about the murders and the attempted killings. However, the head of a security firm who orchestrated the carefully planned gangland executions was jailed for life in May 2009. Bobby Speirs, 41, had the perfect alibi for the attempted murders as he sat in an executive box at Old Trafford in Manchester watching the same match that was on the television in the Brass Handles pub. Using his mobile phone, he planned a calculated demise of a gang rival. He aroused suspicion when he fled the country within days of the murders, but the fact that his gang members failed in their attempts to kill Speirs' rival helped lead to his eventual capture and conviction. It was proved that his phone linked him to the shootings and he was jailed for a minimum of 23 years for conspiracy to murder in an attempted professional gangland execution.

A known Moss Side gangster who was in the pub at the time of the shootings was suspected of firing at the killers with their own weapons once they were overpowered by other drinkers. It was believed that Speirs had recruited the boss of the notorious Doddington gang from south Manchester.

Boss, Ian McLeod, 44, was sentenced to life imprisonment at Preston Crown Court just one year after the gangland attack. Constance Howarth, 40, the woman accused of being the "spotter" in the pub – watching the target, Totton, and directing the gang from her mobile phone – was also jailed for life. Speirs was extradited from Spain to face trial and was told by the judge that he was an extremely dangerous man.